OWN IT

OWN IT

Oprah Winfrey in Her Own Words

Edited by ANJALI BECKER and JEANNE ENGELMANN

AN AGATE IMPRINT

CHICAGO

Printed in the United States

Own It
ISBN-13: 978-1-57284-203-8
ISBN-10: 1-57284-203-2
First printing: October 2016

Libaray of Congress Cataloging-in-Publication Data has
been applied for.

10 9 8 7 6 5 4 3 2 1   17 18 19 20 21

B2 is an imprint of Agate Publishing. Agate books are
available in bulk at discount prices.

agatepublishing.com

"*[The show is] going to do well. And if it doesn't, I will still do well. I will do well, because I am not defined by a show. I think we are defined by the way we treat ourselves and the way we treat other people. It would be wonderful to be acclaimed as this talk show host who's made it, that would be wonderful. But if that doesn't happen, there are other important things in my life.*"

—OPRAH WINFREY, INTERVIEWED BY MIKE WALLACE IN 1986 FOR *60 MINUTES*

TABLE OF CONTENTS

CHALLENGES 35

INTRODUCTION

On May 25th, 2011, the last episode of *The Oprah Winfrey Show* aired to an estimated audience of 16.4 million viewers. For its host, the date marked the conclusion of what had been a largely triumphant 25-year run as one of the most successful talk shows in television history. The "Farewell Season" had been filled with flashbacks to favorite moments from previous years, special reunion episodes, a sit-down with President Barack Obama and First Lady Michelle Obama, and a trip to Australia for 300 lucky viewers. The two-part penultimate episode had been filmed in Chicago's United Center in front of a 13,000-strong crowd and featured appearances from Beyoncé, Madonna, Tom Hanks, Maria Shriver, Tom Cruise, and other notable figures.

Despite, or perhaps because of, all the hoopla surrounding the countdown, the final episode itself was a restrained affair. There were no guest interviews. Instead, Oprah spoke from the heart to her audience, thanking them for going on this journey with her. It was a very personal, completely fitting end, reminding viewers just why Oprah has resonated with so many people over the course of her career.

The cultural impact of *The Oprah Winfrey Show* cannot be overstated and even came to have a name: the Oprah Effect. Products mentioned on *The Oprah Winfrey Show* sold out. Books featured on Oprah's Book Club were catapulted to bestseller lists. The show launched the careers of frequent Oprah guests such as Dr. Phil, Dr. Oz, and Rachael Ray, among others. At its peak, *The Oprah Winfrey Show* averaged over 12 million viewers in the United States and was syndicated in 150 countries around the world.

None of this would have been possible with a different host. Oprah Winfrey is a success because she understands how the power of television can be used to connect with an audience in a fundamentally personal way. Her genius lay in recognizing that people, especially women, would respond to someone to whom they could relate, who they believed understood their own lives and empathized with their struggles. Her authenticity and empathy are two reasons why she has consistently been named as one of America's "most admired" women.

While Oprah does not like to refer to herself as a businesswoman, the fact remains that she has been able to create a media juggernaut based solely on her ability to relate to her audience. Simply put, Oprah's brand is herself. Viewers trusted Oprah's judgment and listened to her recommendations, from soap brands to presidential candidates. Because Oprah took control of *The Oprah Winfrey Show* early on in the show's run, a move that at the time was considered incredibly risky, she was able to reap the financial windfall that came with the show's continued success. Oprah believed wholeheartedly in herself and her ability to understand what the viewing public wanted. The gamble paid off in a major way, turning her into the world's first female African American billionaire and making the Oprah brand one of the most powerful in media.

Since the show debuted in 1984, Oprah has been named to multiple "most powerful" lists, won Emmy Awards, been nominated for the Academy Award, and was awarded the Presidential Medal of Freedom by President Obama in 2013. However, all of this success stands in sharp contrast to Oprah's notoriously difficult early years. Born out of wedlock to a teenage mother in rural Mississippi in 1954, Oprah grew up on a farm in extreme poverty with her maternal grandmother. Years later, she would recall watching her grandmother do laundry and thinking to herself, "I wasn't going to have [this] life."

At age six, Oprah joined her mother Vernita in Milwaukee, Wisconsin. The next few years would be rocky: raped at nine and molested for years by relatives and a family friend, she attempted to run away at 13 and by 14 became pregnant. When the baby died shortly after childbirth, Oprah's father Vernon Winfrey told her she had been given a second chance at life. She moved in with him in Nashville, Tennessee, where she began to thrive, eventually landing a job at Nashville's WLAC-TV. There, she was both the first black female anchor and the youngest.

Oprah moved to Baltimore in 1976 to co-anchor the evening news, but after some difficulties found a position as a talk show co-host, which fit her personality much better. Oprah moved to Chicago in 1983 to take over the half-hour morning talk show *AM Chicago*. Within months, *AM Chicago* was outperforming *The Phil Donahue Show*, then Chicago's highest-rated talk show. In 1985, the show was renamed *The Oprah Winfrey Show*. Due to the early success of her show and the recognition she received for her role in Steven Spielberg's *The Color Purple* (1985), Oprah was able to renegotiate her contract and retain the lucrative syndication rights to the show, which went national in 1986. Oprah formed her production company, Harpo, that same year, and in 1988, Harpo took full control of *The Oprah Winfrey Show*, making Oprah the first woman in history to own her own talk show.

In 1998, she invested in the female-focused Oxygen Network, which floundered and was eventually sold. Later, she said her mistake with Oxygen was not having enough input in the network's direction.

In late 2007, David Zaslav, the CEO of Discovery Communications, came to Oprah with the idea of creating her own network. After some persuasion, she committed, contributing her brand (including oprah.com), her time, and her extensive back catalogue of shows in exchange for a 50-50-ownership stake with Discovery, with Oprah as chairwoman.

OWN launched in January 2011; it averaged 505,000 viewers the first week (in contrast to the seven million daily viewers for *The Oprah Winfrey Show* at the end of its run). The channel continued to struggle and five months after the launch, OWN announced that Oprah herself would take over as CEO and chief creative officer (in addition to her role as chairwoman) in an effort to right the ship. It was a tough year for OWN, with layoffs as well as a reported loss of $330 million for Discovery Communications. Oprah later told *The Hollywood Reporter*, "I had become so accustomed to succeeding that I no longer even remembered what it was like to fail."

In 2012, OWN struck a deal with African American writer–producer Tyler Perry to create several original scripted programs, which have consistently drawn OWN's highest average audience numbers and broadened the network's appeal to African American women in particular. Additionally, exclusive, high-profile interviews with disgraced cyclist Lance Armstrong and with the family of deceased singer Whitney Houston drew millions of viewers and reminded the world that Oprah is one of its most prolific interviewers. In July 2013, OWN reported that it had broken even, beating analyst predictions and reversing the tide of negative headlines.

Despite OWN's early struggles, Oprah's lasting contribution to our culture remains. She has indelibly changed the fabric of daytime television and encouraged her viewers to open up about themselves and their struggles and inspired them to reach for the lives they want to live. The Oprah Winfrey Leadership Academy for Girls, which she opened in South Africa in 2007, has helped girls from disadvantaged backgrounds graduate high school and continue on to college. OWN continues to post positive growth. Its continued success, like her other triumphs, depends on Oprah—and the self-reliance, values, and vision on which she has built her empire.

Previous books in this series referred to the subjects by their last names, following journalistic standards, but Oprah's brand is so synonymous with her first name that we will refer to her as such throughout the book. We hope reading Oprah's words helps you find the wisdom and inspiration to live your own best life.

PREPARATION

••

Your Resume Is Your Story

The challenge of life, I have found, is to build a resume that doesn't simply tell a story about what you want to be, but it's a story about who you want to be. It's a resume that doesn't just tell a story about what you want to accomplish, but why. A story that's not just a collection of titles and positions, but a story that's really about your purpose.

—Harvard Commencement, May 30, 2013

••

Luck

I don't believe in luck. For me, luck is preparation meeting the moment of opportunity. There is no luck without you being prepared to handle that moment of opportunity.

—*Oprah's Master Class*, March 27, 2011

••

Don't Waste Time

What's the smartest thing to do after learning what makes you tick? Answer: waste zero time getting started on living your best life.

—*O, The Oprah Magazine*, August 2015

••

Finding Your Life's Work

Your life's work is to find your life's work—and then to exercise the discipline, tenacity and hard work it takes to pursue it.

—*O, The Oprah Magazine*, September 2001

••

Paying Your Dues

[*SNL* producer Lorne Michaels told me that] this thing that you've taken on is huge. It's big. And nobody wants to see you sashay from the set of *The Oprah Winfrey Show* into this new business and [have] everything go okay. You're going to have to pay your dues, you're going to have to learn the hard way.

—*Oprah Builds a Network*, July 8, 2012

Being Present

I have learned that your full-on attention for any activity you choose to experience comes with a level of intensity and truth. It's about living a present life, moment to moment—not worrying about what's going to happen at 3 o'clock and what's going to happen at 7 o'clock.

—*Fast Company*, October 12, 2015

Being Yourself

When I first started out . . . I was pretending to be somebody I was not. I was pretending to be Barbara Walters. So I'd go to a news conference, and I was more interested in how I phrased the question and how eloquent the question sounded, as opposed to listening to the answer. Which always happens when you are interested in impressing people instead of doing what you are supposed to be doing.

—Academy of Achievement, February 21, 1991

• •

Empowering People Face-to-Face

I'm now understanding that your energy, your es-
sence, your juice cannot be instilled unless you're actually there. You have to be in it first, then you have
to empower everybody else to at least know what
the vision is in such a way that they can execute it.

—*Oprah Builds a Network*, July 8, 2012

• •

Legacy

Your legacy is made every day. . . . Every person that
you encounter in the space of your life [whom] you
impact . . . in any way—that will be your legacy.

—interview with Facebook COO Sheryl Sandberg,
October 2, 2011

· ·

Running Your Own Race

The way you step up your game is not to worry about the other guy in any situation, because you can't control the other guy. You only have control over yourself. So it's like running a race. The energy that it takes to look back and see where the other guys are takes energy away from you. . . . Don't waste your time in the race looking back to see where the other guy is or what the other guy is doing. It's not about the other guy. It's about what can you do.

—*Oprah's Master Class*, March 27, 2011

· ·

Staying True To Yourself

Don't let people talk you into what they think is you.

—The *Hollywood Reporter*, December 11, 2013

• •

Expectations

I remember my father saying to me, "You can't bring Cs in this house because you are not a C student. . . . You are an A student. So that's what we expect in this house." It was just so matter of fact. And I knew he was not faking it one bit. I never even tried to bring in a C because I realized that it's just not acceptable.

—Academy of Achievement, February 21, 1991

• •

Success Flows from Service

The key is not to worry about being successful but to instead work toward being significant—and the success will naturally follow. How can you serve your way to greatness?

—O, The Oprah Magazine, September 2001

• •

Clarity of Purpose

Don't expect the clarity to come all at once, to know your purpose right away.

—Harvard Commencement, May 30, 2013

• •

Choosing Positive People

My greatest advice to you is to surround yourself
with people who are going to fill your cup until
your cup runneth over.

—Spelman College Commencement, May 20, 2012

• •

Learning from Your Own Life

Your life is your greatest teacher. Every single
thing that's happening to you every day: your joys,
your sadnesses, your challenges, your worries. . . .
Everything is trying to take you home to yourself.
And when you're at home with yourself. . . . you
are your best.

—interview at Stanford Graduate School of Business,
April 16, 2014

• •

Your Career Is Not Your Life

As I often tell my girls [attending the Oprah Winfrey Leadership Academy for Girls] from atop my
"Mom O" perch, a career is not a life. What you
want to do should emerge from who you want to
be. *Who do you want to be?* That, to me, is the es-
sential question.

—*O, The Oprah Magazine*, April 2014

••

Patience

All success comes with patience, and with patience comes power.

—The Hollywood Reporter, December 19, 2012

••

What Goes Around

I live by the third law of motion in physics, which is for every action there is an equal and opposite reaction. . . . I know that what I'm thinking, and therefore [what I am] going to act on, is going to come back to me in a circular motion, just like gravity, like what goes up comes down. And so what also propels the action is the intention. So I don't do anything without being fully clear about why I intend to do it. Because the intention is going to determine the reaction, the result, or the consequence in every circumstance.

—interview at Stanford Graduate School of Business, April 16, 2014

• •

You Are Your Own Best Thing

No matter what triumphs, defeats, sad times, painful times, whatever you have to go through in life—you are your own best thing.

—New York Times, May 24, 2011

• •

Nothing Is Guaranteed

I'm keenly aware that every day is a gift, that time is fleeting. Another year has passed. So quickly gone. No moment but this one is guaranteed, so I'm ready to be in each as the healthiest, strongest, fittest, most conscious, most alive me I've ever been.

—O, The Oprah Magazine, January 2016

• •

Choosing Who You Want to Be

Everything I do—my work on TV, my engagement with my school [The Oprah Winfrey Leadership Academy for Girls], my interactions with business partners and personal friends—arises from who I choose to be. And daily, we each get to choose. . . . What kind of person do you want to be?

—O, The Oprah Magazine, April 2014

• •

Listening to Yourself

You understand that when you know better, you ought to do better—and doing better sometimes means changing your mind; and you realize that letting go of what others think you should do is the only way to reach your full potential.

—O, The Oprah Magazine, June 2001

• •

How to Negotiate

Start with clarity of intention. Know yours and your opponent's. Make every deal a win-win. Otherwise, you lose long term.

—The Hollywood Reporter, December 10, 2015

• •

What Successful People Have in Common

Every time we have seen a person on this stage who [has] success in their life, they spoke of the joy and they spoke of the juice that they receive from doing what they knew they were meant to be doing.

—The Oprah Winfrey Show, May 25, 2011

Knowing What You Don't Want

Knowing what you *don't* want to do is the best possible place to be . . . because knowing what you don't want to do leads you to figure out what it is you really do want to do.

—interview at Stanford Graduate School of Business,
April 16, 2014

Questioning Yourself

Let me ask you something: Have you ever posed a question to yourself that shifted your point of view? Maybe, *Is this what I really want?* or *What's my next move?* Over the years, I've asked myself many questions like these, from *What do I know for sure? . . .* to *What am I doing that's working? . . .* I've learned that big-picture pondering can have life-changing effects.

—*O, The Oprah Magazine*, April 2014

· ·

Your Past Informs Your Present

Every single thing that's ever happened to you has happened . . . to make you who you are in this moment right now. And *who* you are in this moment right now is all you need to keep standing and to keep moving forward.

—interview with Facebook COO Sheryl Sandberg,

October 2, 2011

RISK-TAKING

• •

Using Your Fear

I asked myself, I actually wrote it down, "What would I do if I wasn't afraid?" And I thought of what all the answers would be. Of course you would have a network. Of course you would build that platform and you would build it digitally and you would speak to the world and you would try to open people's hearts and you would let them see the best of themselves. That's what I would do if I wasn't afraid. . . . So I said, "Pretend you're not afraid and then take that step," and that is what I did.

— interview with Facebook COO Sheryl Sandberg,
October 2, 2011

● ●

Owning Your Future

In her first year in Chicago, Oprah asked her bosses at WLS for two months off to film Steven Spielberg's The Color Purple, *but her contract only allotted her two weeks off per year. Instead, she was made to give up future time off for the next several years in order to film. After the movie's success and the success of her own talk show, Oprah was able to renegotiate her contract.*

You never want to be in a position where something is that important to you to do, and you can't do it because the boss says you can't. You want to be able to own yourself and make your own decisions about what's important to you to do. . . . So the fact that I had not been allowed the time [to film] *The Color Purple* is the reason why I made the decision to take the risk to own my own show. And that has made all the difference in the trajectory of my career.

—speech at Stanford University, April 20, 2015

. . . .

Taking Advantage of Change

If change is the one thing you can be sure of, the goal is to figure out how you can use that certainty to your advantage, to modify, transfigure, refashion, and transform your day-to-day being.

—*O, The Oprah Magazine*, September 2014

. . . .

Being Flexible

What I know for sure is that the only way to endure the quake is to adjust your stance. You can't avoid the daily tremors. They come with being alive. But I believe these experiences are gifts that force us to step to the right or left in search of a new center of gravity. Don't fight them. Let them help you adjust your footing.

—*What I Know For Sure*, p. 35

• •

Not Playing It Safe

Oprah was deeply unhappy while working at WJZ-TV in Baltimore early in her career. She left to host the struggling morning show AM Chicago, *which would become a success almost overnight and was later renamed* The Oprah Winfrey Show.

Staying in Baltimore would have been the safe thing to do. But sitting in my boss's office, I knew that if I let him talk me into staying, it would affect the way I felt about myself forever. I would always wonder what could have been. That one choice changed the trajectory of my life.

—*What I Know For Sure*, p. 125

• •

Doing What Is Necessary

I knew that the three of us [Oprah along with OWN co-Presidents Sheri Salata and Erik Logan] would have to join forces to lead our team to success. Even if that meant that we would have to go out into the field and be "boots to the ground" as new series started shooting. Whatever it took, we would have to do it.

—*Oprah Builds a Network*, July 8, 2012

Recalibrating

We live in a state of constant change. Whether or not we're paying attention, the process is always happening. . . . Life is about recalibrating. About continually asking yourself: *What do I have to do to get where I need to be? How do I create the life I want?*

—*O, The Oprah Magazine*, September 2014

Speaking Out

If I can't take a risk, nobody can. What I have decided is that with fame, notoriety, credibility, if you can't have the courage then to stand up and speak out for what you truly believe in, then it means nothing.

—*Vogue*, October 1998

You're Not Alone

When you see other people who have come through the worst, who have survived what you're going through, it lets you know you can.

—*Makers: Women Who Make America*,
February 26, 2013

• •

No Free Rides

You can't know who you are when you spend too much time on the mountaintop. You have to be taken down from the mountain in order to rise to the next level. There's no way you can accomplish anything of any value without having a challenge. Nobody just rides into anything. Nobody.

—*Oprah Builds a Network*, July 15, 2012

• •

Setting Trends

At the conclusion of its 25-year-run, Oprah reminisced on the early topics of The Oprah Winfrey Show*:*

We were living it and doing it and being a part of all the experiences we were showing. Girls in the office were looking for men so we did a show about how to find a good man. One of the producers had AIDS so we started doing shows about that. We didn't have a finger on the pulse, we *were* the pulse.

—*New York Times*, May 24, 2011

· ·

Being the Boss

We became a syndicated show in 1986. So I went in to the bosses and I said, "My team, they need to make more money." And the boss at the time said, "Why? You're all girls." That moment in the office, that was a deciding factor for me. I came back and said, "Look, I want to own my own show, and I want to take the risk of owning my own show," so that I [would] be the one to say who gets what paycheck.

—*Makers: Women Who Make America*,
February 26, 2013

· ·

Enjoying the Journey

The greatest lesson from that experience [making the film *Beloved*] is to do your best, enjoy the journey, and then release all attachment to what is to come. Let it be. And be comfortable with whatever it is.

—*O, The Oprah Magazine*, February 2001

• •

Learning from Challenges

There's no question that changing the way you think about your situation is the key to improving it. I know for sure that all of our hurdles have meaning. And being open to learning from those challenges is the difference between succeeding and getting stuck.

—*What I Know For Sure*, p. 44

• •

Midlife Crisis

There's been a lot written lately about midlife depression. Suddenly, midlifers have so many options. Their children are grown and they're asking themselves, "What do I do now? Who am I?" They're looking at the possibility of a second life, at reinventing themselves.

—*USA Today*, March 2, 2008

• •

Asking for It

Here's what I've learned: If you don't ask for it, you're not likely to get it.

—*O, The Oprah Magazine*, July 2014

· ·

Moving On

In every job I've taken and every city in which I've lived, I have known that it's time to move on when I've grown as much as I can. Sometimes moving on terrified me. But always it taught me that the true meaning of courage is to be afraid, and then, with your knees knocking, to step out anyway.

—*What I Know For Sure*, p. 103

DECISION-MAKING

∙∙∙

Finding Your Purpose

What I know for sure is that the biggest choices begin and end with you—your internal big questions: Who do I want to be in the world?

—Spelman College Commencement, May 20, 2012

∙∙∙

Knowing When to Quit

When [my producers] called me in and said, "I know, we could take the audience to outer space," I knew it was time to go.

—*The Hollywood Reporter*, December 11, 2013

∙∙∙

Honoring Yourself

When you honor what you know your spirit is telling you to do, you are making the most conscientious decision, one for which you are willing to accept all the consequences.

—*O, The Oprah Magazine*, June 2001

••

Layoffs

In early 2012, OWN laid off around 30 employees and canceled Rosie O'Donnell's much-hyped talk show The Rosie Show *in an effort to restructure the company.*

I think of every employee as a person first, as a human being with a family. We had many conversations about where we were as a company and how we were going to be able to sustain ourselves. And I knew from the time I stepped in as CEO [in July 2011] and started to sit in those meetings and look at the real numbers on the page, that the only way through is you're either going to have to end it, or you're going to have to make some cutbacks now so you'll be able to go forward. So the idea of having to let 30 people go, that was really rough. That was a tough decision.

—*Oprah Builds a Network*, July 15, 2012

••

Listening to Your Instincts

I have from the very beginning listened to my instinct. All of my best decisions in life have come because I was attuned to what really felt like the next right move for me.

—interview at Stanford Graduate School of Business,
April 16, 2014

. . . .

Strategic-Planning Meetings

If I called a strategic-planning meeting, there would be dead silence, and then people would fall out of their chairs laughing.

—Fortune, April 1, 2002

. . . .

Asking the Right Questions

What I know for sure, sitting high atop the perch of broader perspective at 60: Whether you're trying to create a great conversation or a great life, it's the questions that count. Ask the right questions, and the answers will always reveal themselves.

—O, The Oprah Magazine, April 2014

. . . .

Multitasking

[Multitasking is] a joke for me. When I try to do that, I don't do anything well.

—Fast Company, October 12, 2015

•••

Listening to Your Uncertainty

I believe that uncertainty is my spirit's way of whispering, *I'm in flux. I can't decide for you. Something is off balance here.* I take that as a cue to re-center myself before making a decision.

—*What I Know For Sure*, p. 176

•••

Waiting for Clarity

When you don't know what to do, my best advice is to do nothing until clarity comes. Getting still, being able to hear your own voice and not the voices of the world, quickens clarity. Once you decide what you want, make a commitment to that decision.

—*What I Know For Sure*, p. 215

•••

Planning Ahead

Once my life was mine to design, I found myself a bit unbalanced in structuring it. I've had to learn to plan what I want to do instead of always fulfilling the "have to dos."

—*O, The Oprah Magazine*, April 2015

Removing Your Fear

Whenever I'm faced with a difficult decision, I ask myself: What would I do if I weren't afraid of making a mistake, feeling rejected, looking foolish, or being alone? I know for sure that when you remove the fear, the answer you've been searching for comes into focus. And as you walk into what you fear, *you* should know for sure that your deepest struggle can, if you're willing and open, produce your greatest strength.

— *What I Know For Sure*, p. 39

Listening to Your Inner Voice

You cannot fulfill [your greater purpose] unless you have a level of self-awareness. [You need] to be connected to what is the inner voice or instinct—I call it the "emotional GPS system"—that allows you to make the best decisions for yourself. And every decision that has profited me has come from me listening to that inner voice first. Every time I have gotten into a situation where I was in trouble, it's because I didn't listen to it.

—interview at Stanford Graduate School of Business, April 16, 2014

CHALLENGES

··

Rough Patches

Ever notice how some of the most eye-opening moments in life occur when the going gets tough? Rough patches are scary, for sure, but they can also be truly transformative.

—*O, The Oprah Magazine*, August 2014

··

There's No Such Thing as Failure

It doesn't matter how far you might rise. At some point, you are bound to stumble because . . . if you are constantly pushing yourself higher [and] higher, the law of averages, not to mention the myth of Icarus, predicts that you will at some point fall. And when you do, I want you to know this, remember this: ~~There is no such thing as failure. Failure is just life trying to move us in another direction.~~

—Harvard Commencement, May 30, 2013

. . . .

Learning from Your Critics

I take criticism very seriously. I can't say that I'm one of those people who does not read criticism because I do. And if someone criticizes something, and it strikes a nerve with me, I will then move to correct it. I have written to critics who said things that I thought were very valid.

—Academy of Achievement, February 21, 1991

. . . .

Mistakes Are Teachable Moments

When you're down in the hole, when that moment comes, it's really okay to feel bad for a little while. Give yourself time to mourn what you think you may have lost. But then—here's the key—learn from every mistake. Because every experience, en-counter, and particularly your mistakes are there to teach you and force you into being more of who you are.

—Harvard Commencement, May 30, 2013

Disagreements

All of [our] arguments are really about the same thing: It's about, "Did you hear me? Did you see me? And did what I say mean anything to you?"

—interview at Stanford Graduate School of Business,
April 16, 2014

Setting Expectations

I also understand that because I had a 25-year reputation that I built, that there was a big expectation [for OWN]. . . . And when we started with this network, I was the only person saying, "Let's not make it big, let's just start small, let's not do a big, big, big, big thing." Because you set an expectation that you cannot live up to. It's better for people to have lower expectations for you to overdeliver [on] rather than to underdeliver.

—*CBS This Morning*, April 2, 2012

· ·

Don't Rest on Your Laurels

I think the expectation—and part of my own expectation—was I had 25 years of success, and I thought
people would just leverage that into the network.
Well, we didn't account for people not having the
channel, not knowing how to find the channel, the
cable audience being different than the broadcast
audience, and more competition.

—*The Hollywood Reporter*, December 19, 2012

· ·

Being Lean

*In 2012, in the midst of OWN's darkest period,
Oprah contrasted the successful launch of her talk
show with the rocky start of OWN.*

My show was built around me and five producers.
I'd go out and get the lunch for us—Taco Bell or
Burger King. I prided myself on leanness. The op-
posite was done here [with OWN].

—*Wall Street Journal*, May 6, 2012

Pleasing Others

Most all the mistakes I've made in my life, I've made because I was trying to please other people. . . . Every mistake I've ever made was because I went outside of myself to do something for somebody else that I should not have.

—Academy of Achievement, February 21, 1991

Maintaining Control

[The failure of Oxygen network] was a great lesson for me: Don't partner when you're not allowed to be in charge and make a decision.

—*New York Times*, December 18, 2010

Schadenfreude

The fact that no matter what you've accomplished . . . you're still susceptible to that kind of schadenfreude was really very helpful to me. So I will move through life differently, more enhanced by that experience of the valley and will be a better businesswoman and better person because of it.

—*Oprah Builds a Network*, July 15, 2012

· ·

Finding Higher Ground

Balance lives in the present. When you feel the earth moving, bring yourself back to the now. You'll handle whatever shake-up the next moment brings when you get to it. In *this* moment, you're still breathing. In *this* moment, you've survived. In *this* moment, you're finding a way to step onto higher ground.

—*What I Know For Sure*, p. 35

· ·

New Directions

One of my greatest lessons has been to fully understand that what looks like a dark patch in the quest for success is the universe pointing you in a new direction.

—*What I Know For Sure*, p. 46

· ·

Stepping Out of Your Ego

I've learned that sometimes you have to step out of your ego to recognize the truth. So when life gets difficult, I've found that the best thing to do is ask myself a simple question: *What is this here to teach me?*

—*What I Know For Sure*, p. 42

· ·

Listening to Life

Life is always speaking to us, especially in our greatest trials. The question is will you listen to the whispers.

—*Ebony*, September 11, 2014

WORK/LIFE BALANCE

Fun

I am really good at working. Committed. Diligent. With stamina on steroids. Playing, I'm not so good at. I rarely decide to do anything just for fun. So the question I've recently started asking myself is, *Am I having a good time?* Am I doing what I really want? What does fun look like?

—*O, The Oprah Magazine*, February 2015

Avoiding Negativity

I try not to waste time—because I don't want to waste myself. I'm working on not letting people with dark energy consume any of my minutes on this earth. I've learned that the hard way, after giving up hours of myself and my time, which are synonymous when you think about it.

—*What I Know For Sure*, p. 186

....

Dysfunction

Over the years I've interviewed thousands of people—most of them women—and I would say that
the root of every dysfunction I've ever encoun-
tered, every problem, has been [from] some sense
of a lacking of self-value or self-worth.

— interview with Michelle Obama, June 14, 2016

....

Learning to Say No

The ability to learn to say "no" and not feel guilty
about it is the greatest success I have achieved. For
me to have the kind of internal strength and internal courage it takes to say, "No, I will not let you
treat me this way," is what success is all about.

—Academy of Achievement, February 21, 1991

....

Time

Just because the phone is ringing doesn't mean I
have to respond. I control what I do with my time.
We all do, even when it seems out of control. Pro-
tect your time. It is your life.

—*What I Know For Sure*, p. 178

• •

Protecting Your Light

I've learned from my experiences of getting sucked into other people's ego dysfunction that their darkness robs you of your own light—the light you need to be for yourself and for others. What I know for sure is that how you spend your time defines who you are. And I want to shine my light for good.

—What I Know For Sure, p. 186

• •

Not Having Children

The reason why I didn't have children and don't regret [not] having children is because the show became my life.

—interview with Barbara Walters, December 9, 2010

• •

Taking Breaks

I began scheduling little moments of calm—moments in which I do nothing for at least ten minutes. . . . Whenever I give myself these little breaks, I find I have more energy, and I'm in a better mood for all the business that comes afterward.

—What I Know For Sure, p. 181

• •

Work Day

A 12-hour day is a short day for me. I feel like, after a 12-hour day, "What am I going to do with the rest of my day?" I get home, and I don't know what to do with myself because I have all of this time left over. I don't know what to do. So I really feel most comfortable working 14 to 16 hours because then, at least, I can go home.

—Academy of Achievement, February 21, 1991

• •

Silence

I crave silence. It's how I balance out the volume that's necessary to run a network and a magazine and remain somewhat sociable. What makes me *me* is being able to return to stillness.

—*O, The Oprah Magazine*, October 2014

• •

Turning Down Requests

Just because you have all of these demands on your time and on you doesn't mean that you have to say yes. . . . Understanding that really changed the meaning of my life in that I was no longer driven by what other people wanted me to do.

—speech at Stanford University, April 20, 2015

●●●

Leaving Space in Your Calendar

Keeping it all straight is stressful. You need to give yourself moments to rest. I once told my assistant that just because I have ten free minutes on my calendar doesn't mean I want to fill them.

—*What I Know For Sure*, p. 180

●●●

Relaxation

Whether you have a week to laze around or a 20-minute break between errands, I promise it's possible to truly relax.

—*O, The Oprah Magazine*, July 2015

●●●

Finding Balance

I work hard and play well; I believe in the yin and yang of life. It doesn't take a lot to make me happy because I find satisfaction in so much of what I do. Some satisfactions are higher-rated than others, of course. And because I try to practice what I preach—living in the moment—I am consciously attuned most of the time to how much pleasure I am receiving.

—*What I Know For Sure*, p. 6

• •

Staying Refreshed

Who couldn't use a little refresh now and again? I'm a big fan of the kinds of minor changes that add up to major delight—a quick swap, a brilliant fix, a more efficient strategy—and I'm betting you are, too.

—*O, The Oprah Magazine*, September 2014

• •

Happiness

I really don't define my happiness by my business decisions.

—*Fortune*, April 1, 2002

• •

Time Management

It will only get worse if you don't learn to manage your time now. And it's yours to design.

—*O, The Oprah Magazine*, June 2015

- -

Fresh Starts

We all get the opportunity to feel wonder every day, but we've been lulled into numbness. Have you ever driven home from work, opened your front door, and asked yourself how you got there? I know for sure that I don't want to live a shut-down life—desensitized to feeling and seeing. I want every day to be a fresh start on expanding what is possible.

—*What I Know For Sure*, p. 24

- -

Prioritizing Yourself

Your primary job is to take care of yourself. You've got to decide to make your health and well-being your priority; otherwise you run out of oxygen.

—*O, The Oprah Magazine*, June 2015

• •

Remembering to Breathe

Ever notice how often you unconsciously hold your breath? Once you start paying attention, it might surprise you to see how much tension you've been carrying around inside. Nothing is more effective than a deep, slow inhale and release for surrendering what you can't control and focusing again on what's right in front of you.

—*What I Know For Sure*, p. 170

• •

Focusing on the Present

I'm not nearly as stressed as people might imagine. Over the years, I've learned to focus my energy on the present, to be fully aware of what's happening in every moment and not to worry about what should have happened, what's going wrong, or what might come next.

—*What I Know For Sure*, p. 167

LEADERSHIP

••

Owning Your Vision

You can have vision but unless you maintain leadership of the vision and are there to help oversee the execution of the vision, it doesn't work.

—*The Hollywood Reporter*, December 19, 2012

••

Pursuing Excellence

Somewhere deep within me, even when I was a teenager, I always sensed that something bigger was in store for me—but it was never about attaining wealth or celebrity. It was about the process of continually seeking to be better, to challenge myself to pursue excellence on every level.

—*What I Know For Sure*, p. 126

••

Humility

I always understood that there really was no difference between me and [my] audience. . . . At the
core of what really matters, we are the same. And
you know how I know that? Because all of us are
seeking the same thing. . . . Everybody wants to
fulfill the highest, truest expression of yourself as
a human being.

—interview at Stanford Graduate School of Business,
April 16, 2014

••

Showing Up

You can't call in sick; you can't ever give less than
100 percent. And if you are sick, which I have been
a couple times, that's when you gotta pull up to 110,
120. Because people have come from all over the
country and this is their moment. They've saved
their money, they've bought their airline tickets,
they've got new outfits, they've called their sisters,
their cousins, their aunts, their mother-in-laws,
their mothers, and that is why they're there, to see
[me]. So I feel a sense of responsibility, a sense of
obligation, a sense of respect, reverence, and honor
for those people.

—interview with Barbara Walters, December 9, 2010

Creating the Culture

I only want the people with me who want to be with me. I only want the people who are in, who buy into the bigger, global mission and vision of what it is we're trying to do. We're not just creating a television network; we weren't just creating shows. And so I have said that is in the culture. You're here because you want to be a part of this big thing, this big and bigger thing that we are doing.

—interview with Facebook COO Sheryl Sandberg,
October 2, 2011

Hiring the Right People

I try to surround myself with people who really know what they're doing and [then] give them the freedom to do it.

—*Fast Company*, October 12, 2015

••

Envisioning the Future

Every farewell offers an opportunity for a new hello.
. . . When one road ends, it's time to look ahead in
a new direction. And know that as far as your eye
can see, the universe can see even farther. That is
where we're headed.

—*O, The Oprah Magazine*, May 2015

••

Sharing Intentions

I literally had a big meeting with all my producers
and I said, "We are now going to become an in-
tentional television show. . . . We are only going to
do shows that come from a motivation that we're
going to show people the best of themselves. . . . But
the idea behind it—the vision—is that we are going
to be a force for good, and that is going to be our
intention."

—interview with LinkedIn CEO Jeff Weiner,
October 15, 2015

• •

Sending a Message

The only reason to be a person whom everybody knows, who is successful, is to transmit the message of successfulness, to say, "That is possible."

—*Makers: Women Who Make America*,
February 26, 2013

• •

Taking Control

[*SNL* producer] Lorne Michaels [told me that] the channel will turn around when you get there, when you are physically present, and you are able to every day allow the words that you say and the vision that you hold to be executed in the way that you see fit. That's when it's going to change. You're going to have to physically put yourself there and you're going to have to physically take control.

—*Oprah Builds a Network*, July 8, 2012

••

Holding High Expectations

I used to do for every employee—now I have 700, so I can't—but I used to do what I call "the gut check." I would just spend a few minutes doing my own emotional check of how I felt about this person, whether I sensed their honesty.

—*The Hollywood Reporter*, November 25, 2007

••

Integrity in Action

People refer to me as a brand now, the "Oprah Brand." I never knew what a brand was when I first started out—I didn't even know what that [meant]. I became a brand by making every decision flow from the truth of myself. Every choice I made, for every show that was going to be on the air, I made based on, "Does this feel right? . . . Is this going to help somebody?"

—*Forbes* 400 Summit on Philanthropy, June 26, 2012

••

Developing Talent

This is what I feel is the key to developing talent. . . . You have to find the thread of authenticity. You have to find what is real. That's the key.

—interview with Barbara Walters, December 9, 2010

· ·

Creating a Team

I've tried to surround myself with people who are all in, fully 100 percent for the next level of this mission, and who understand that it's not about creating more television shows. It's about connecting and speaking to the world in such a way that people . . . can begin to see the best of themselves. So we become a mirror to show them the best of themselves. And that is by carefully . . . selecting and gathering the tribe to [myself] of people who want to be a part of that mission.

—interview with Facebook COO Sheryl Sandberg,
October 2, 2011

· ·

Working Together

When you are in a foxhole, you have to surround yourself with people who can help lift you out.

—*CBS This Morning*, August 5, 2013

....

Sharing the Load

We now need 8,000 hours to fill a network. So I have to build the team. I'm in the process of taking the team that worked with me for 25 years on the *Oprah* show and combining that team with the team at OWN in Los Angeles to create a force so that it's not just me looking at all the shows and me making every decision . . . I am one person and cannot do all of that.

—interview with Facebook COO Sheryl Sandberg,
October 2, 2011

....

Courage

Bravery shows up in everyday life when people have the courage to live their truth, their vision, and their dreams.

—*O, The Oprah Magazine*, January 2015

Personal Growth

Soon after I started the show, something shifted for me, it really did. I started the show as a job, and was very happy to get the job. But it was not long before I understood that there was something else going on here, more than just job satisfaction. Something in me connected with each of you in a way that allowed me to see myself in you, and you in me. I listened and grew, and I know you grew along with me. Sometimes, I was a teacher, and more often, you taught me. It is no coincidence that I always wanted to be a teacher, and I ended up in the world's biggest classroom.

—*The Oprah Winfrey Show*, May 25, 2011

Raising Consciousness

My real contribution—the reason why I'm here—is to help connect people to themselves and the higher ideas of consciousness. . . . So my television platform was to help raise consciousness.

—interview at Stanford Graduate School of Business,
April 16, 2014

• •

Honesty under Fire

This is what leadership is all about. To use your voice, no matter what the personal consequences, so that abuse will end and good will prevail.

—Oprah Winfrey Leadership Academy for Girls,
November 5, 2007

• •

Shared Vision, Shared Passion

The real key is not making emotional decisions . . . [it's] starting with the infrastructure and the leadership that can sustain [projects] long term. . . . You have to have people whose vision is not only aligned with yours, but they also carry the passion for the vision as you do. . . . You need people who are equally as passionate about it as you are, and when you can do that, then you at least have a chance.

—*Forbes* 400 Summit on Philanthropy, June 26, 2012

Figuring Out What Works

Everybody who is going to lead anything in their life—whether you're running your house, whether you're running multiple businesses—for a lot of that work, it's a guessing game. And it's really a guessing game until you can figure out, as we are still trying to do [with OWN], what is going to best serve [your] audience.

—*Oprah Builds a Network*, July 8, 2012

Meetings

[I] really, really, really try to avoid meetings.

—*Fast Company*, October 12, 2015

Thinking Big

Playing small doesn't serve me. The truth is, I want millions of people. I'm not one of those people who says, "Oh, if I change just one person's life . . ." Nope, not satisfied with just a few. I want millions of people!

—*Fortune*, September 30, 2010

· ·

Running a Business

The biggest mistake in the beginning was not understanding that you need infrastructure and systems in order to run a business. And that there's a reason why there's a hierarchy in reporting systems in business. You can't handle a business like friendship.

— *The Hollywood Reporter*, November 25, 2007

· ·

Fostering Hope

You first have to change the way a person thinks and sees themselves. So you've gotta create a sense of aspiration, a sense of hopefulness, so a person can see, can begin to even have a vision for a better life.

—interview at Stanford Graduate School of Business, April 16, 2014

· ·

Putting the Right People in Charge

One of the lessons I learned from my school is that the same person it takes to build a school isn't the same person to carry on the school.

— *The Hollywood Reporter*, May 26, 2011

Intention

The number one principle that rules my life is intention.

—interview with LinkedIn CEO Jeff Weiner,
October 15, 2015

Leading by Example

Become the change you want to see—those are words I live by. Instead of belittling, uplift. Instead of demolishing, rebuild. Instead of misleading, light the way so that all of us can stand on higher ground.

—*What I Know For Sure*, p. 200

Serving Others

I would ask [my producers on the show] that my voice, the words that I [choose], come from a place that is centered, and centered in the desire to be a force for good and connect in a way that would be meaningful to people.

—interview with LinkedIn CEO Jeff Weiner,
October 15, 2015

··

Taking Responsibility

The *buck* always stops with me.

—Oprah Winfrey Leadership Academy for Girls,
November 5, 2007

··

Trusting Your People

I want to surround myself with people who are smarter than I am about what they do, particularly if it comes to technology and computers, because I can't get the damn TV on! I want them to do their jobs. And I want to give them the freedom and the allowance to do it as well as possible.

—*Entertainment Weekly*, May 6, 2011

··

Self Reflection

I know that one of the things that is so important for what happens here at the Graduate School, is that you have leaders who are self-actualized and understand what your contribution to change the world can be. You can only do that if you know yourself. You cannot do that unless you take the time to actually know who you are and why you are here.

—interview at Stanford Graduate School of Business,
April 16, 2014

Leading Through Transitions

Saying farewell [to Harpo Studios and *The Oprah Winfrey Show*] was sobering, emotional and hard. It was also necessary. We had the greatest run in television history, but it was time to be realistic about going forward. About *growing* forward.

—*O, The Oprah Magazine*, May 2015

Sharing Opportunity

I love giving people opportunities where there might not have been one. Because somebody did that for me.

—*Variety*, October 6, 2015

• •

Leveraging Your Strengths

What I want you to know as this show ends [is that] each one of you has your own platform. Do not let the trappings here fool you. Mine is a stage in a studio; yours is wherever you are, with your own reach. However small or however large that reach is, maybe it's 20 people, maybe it's 30 people, 40 people, your family, your friends, your neighbors, your classmates, your classroom, your coworkers. Wherever you are—that is your platform, your stage, your circle of influence. That is your talk show, and that is where your power lies.

—*The Oprah Winfrey Show*, May 25, 2011

MISSION, VISION, AND PHILANTHROPY

. . . .

Inspiring Others with Your Mission

People tell me the reason they stay here is because of . . . me. And also because of the mission. A vast majority of the people understands that we're not just doing television and haven't been for quite some time. And a vast majority of the people [are] here because of the principles by which we do television.

—*The Hollywood Reporter*, November 25, 2007

. . . .

Service to Others

Develop a new vision of service to others, to your family, community, and world. Lift yourself out of the mundane to magnificent heights. If you honor your calling, your life will be blessed.

—Kellogg School of Management convocation address, June 16, 2001

. . . .

Sharing Your Vision

Everybody who works here at Harpo considers it a gift to have been able to serve all of you, our viewers. I have said many times that I have the best team in TV, and it's not just because they're great at what they do, not just because they work 17-hour days . . . it's because we all here are aligned with the vision of service to you, our viewers.

—The Oprah Winfrey Show, May 25, 2011

. . . .

Finding Your Calling

This is what I was called to do. What I know for sure from this experience with you is that we all are called. Everybody has a calling, and your real job in life is to figure out what that is and get about the business of doing it.

—The Oprah Winfrey Show, May 25, 2011

. . . .

Developing a Platform

For a long time, I thought it was just a job. . . . [It was] around '88 or '89 that I started to see, oh this is bigger than television, that it's actually a platform.

—interview with LinkedIn CEO Jeff Weiner,
October 15, 2015

Following Your Own Lead

The way to be of service is to answer the call for yourself—what is it you want to do and you want to give?—not to be confused by the voices of the world telling you what you're supposed to do.

—interview with Facebook COO Sheryl Sandberg,
October 2, 2011

Brand

I always personalize [things] because that is my brand. For me, everything is personal.

—*Forbes* 400 Summit on Philanthropy, June 26, 2012

OWN's Philosophy

I don't think the world needs another television channel. What the world needs is a different way of looking at itself. What the world needs is inspiration and light and exhilaration and stimulation and a little joy. What we need is to be able to look at the best of ourselves . . . instead of the lowest common denominator that so many television shows program to.

—interview with Facebook COO Sheryl Sandberg,
October 2, 2011

••

Education Is Liberation

Education is what liberated me. The ability to read saved my life. I would have been an entirely different person had I not been taught to read when I was at an early age. My entire life experience, my ability to believe in myself, and even in my darkest moments of sexual abuse and being physically abused and so forth, I knew there was another way. I knew there was a way out. I knew there was another kind of life because I'd read about it.

—Academy of Achievement, February 21, 1991

••

Doing Comes from Being

I think philanthropy should come out of you: Your doing should come out of your being.

—interview at Stanford Graduate School of Business,
April 16, 2014

....

Having Vision

[It's about] understanding the greater vision, purpose, and calling of whatever your philanthropic efforts are [and] holding on to what you really intended—what is the larger vision for what you're trying to do? It's what Stephen Covey has often called "beginning with the end in mind." Holding the end in mind is what has gotten me through every crisis, either [in] business or philanthropically.

—*Forbes* 400 Summit on Philanthropy, June 26, 2012

....

Changing Lives

The greatest thing about what I do, for me, is that I'm in a position to change people's lives. It is the most incredible platform for influence that you could imagine, and it's something that I hold in great esteem and take full responsibility for.

—Academy of Achievement, February 21, 1991

....

Surrendering to Your Dream

All of us need a vision for our lives. . . . Success comes when you surrender to that dream—and let it lead you to the next best place.

—*O, The Oprah Magazine*, September 2001

• •

Living in the Moment

I live in the moment. People are saying to me, how are you going to top this? It's not my desire to top it, my desire is to keep manifesting for myself the life I was meant to live, and so that could take me anywhere.

—*People*, May 30, 2005

• •

What Really Matters

We're all confused about fame versus service in this country.

—*The Oprah Winfrey Show*, May 25, 2011

• •

Lightening Up

On whether her decision to spoof her brand and network on Jimmy Kimmel Live! *was risky:*

Are you kidding? If you can't laugh at yourself. . . . This is what people need to get about this whole brand thing: My heart is my brand. . . . Wherever I am, and [wherever] my heart is, therein lies my brand. My heart is never going to be tarnished. My heart is never going to be ruined. My heart is never going to be taken down.

—*Oprah Builds a Network*, July 8, 2012

. . . .

Sharing

Life is better when you share it.

—*Forbes* 400 Summit on Philanthropy, June 26, 2012

. . . .

Being Kind

Extend yourself in kindness to other human beings wherever you can.

—Harvard Commencement, May 30, 2013

. . . .

Female Education

When you invest in a girl, you change a community. . . . In every study that's ever been done, if a woman is educated, if a girl is educated, she's going to educate her children. If a girl is educated . . . she's more likely to have fewer children. She's more likely to use protection, to take care of herself and her children. She's more likely to then take what she knows and share that with her entire community.

—interview with Facebook COO Sheryl Sandberg,
October 2, 2011

● ●

Feminism

Regarding her early life:

I never did consider or call myself a feminist, but I don't think you can really be a woman in this world and not be.

—*Makers: Women Who Make America,*
February 26, 2013

● ●

Civil Rights Movement

I am a student of the Civil Rights movement. I understand very clearly that I get to sit in the seat that I hold in life because there are a lot of people who paved the way for me.

—*Live with Kelly and Michael,* December 19, 2014

Gratitude

My heart overflows with gratitude to the people who stuck by me when the critics had called it quits for me and my "struggling" network. I grew to disdain the word *struggle* every time I saw it written to describe our state of affairs. But then I started to replace the narrative with gratitude. "I'm so grateful to have this opportunity to speak to the world in this way." . . . "I'm so grateful to be able to speak with a voice that's relevant to the issues of our times." When I shifted the paradigm to giving thanks, the work itself shifted.

—*O, The Oprah Magazine*, December 2013

Finding Your Passion

Have the courage to follow your passion—and if you don't know what it is, realize that one reason for your existence on earth is to find it.

—*O, The Oprah Magazine*, September 2001

. . . .

Philanthropy

We're all trying to be here on the planet and fulfill what it is our heart wants to express. When you can figure out a thing that connects with you, there really isn't anything better. I feel expanded because of the work that I do that's called charity.

—Variety, October 6, 2015

. . . .

Material Success

What other people view as successful is not what my idea of success is. And I don't mean to belittle it at all. It's really nice to be able to have nice things. What material success does is provide you with the ability to concentrate on other things that really matter. And that is being able to make a difference, not only in your own life, but in other people's lives.

—Academy of Achievement, February 21, 1991

Education Opens Doors

[Education matters] because it's an open door to a real life, and you can't get through this life without it and succeed. It's an open door to discovery and wonder and fascination and figuring out who you are, why you're here, and what you came to do. It's an invitation to life, and it feeds you forever.

—*Variety*, October 6, 2015

Recognizing When You've Made It

How do you know whether you're on the right path, with the right person, or in the right job? The same way you know when you're not. You feel it.

—*O, The Oprah Magazine*, September 2001

Books

When you educate a woman, you set her free. Had I not had books and education in Mississippi, I would have believed that's all there was.

—*Fortune*, April 1, 2002

∙∙

Inspiration

You first have to change the way a person thinks and sees themselves. So you've gotta create a sense of aspiration, a sense of hopefulness, so a person can see, can begin to even have a vision for a better life.

—interview at Stanford Graduate School of Business,
April 16, 2014

∙∙

We Are All Alike

I think part of our dysfunction in this country comes [from a feeling] that everybody else's life is happier than ours. What the talk shows—ours and Phil Donahue's and a few others—serve to show is that, really, we are all more alike than we are different, and none of us are like June Cleaver. I think we dismantled a lot of that.

—*Vogue*, October 1998

OWN's Mission

I believe people want to see television that is fun, that is entertaining, but that is also meaningful. What I want to do is use it as a platform for transforming people's lives . . . but if I see that that's not what the audience wants, then I will move on to the next thing.

—*CBS This Morning*, April 2, 2012

Giving Your Truth

You can be the kind of person who writes the biggest check and think nothing else about it, and you do it because that's good for your portfolio or it's good for a tax write-off, or you can be the kind of person who doesn't have a lot to give, but reaches inside to the truth in the core of yourself, and you give that. And that person is rewarded exponentially.

—*Forbes* 400 Summit on Philanthropy, June 26, 2012

• •

Empowering Others

One of my true roles on Earth is to be an inspiration and to help people to connect to ideas that inspire and expand their vision of who they can be in the world. . . . My role is to break down big ideas about who we are in a way that people can see it and taste it and feel it and know it for themselves.

—interview with LinkedIn CEO Jeff Weiner,
October 15, 2015

• •

Changing Perspectives

Nothing makes me happier in my work—still to this day, if there's something in our magazine and someone writes and says, "You know, I read this article and I never thought of it this way before." [Those are] my favorite words.

—*Forbes* 400 Summit on Philanthropy, June 26, 2012

• •

Providing Inspiration

I feel that my role here on earth is to inspire people, and to get them to look at themselves.

—*Fast Company*, October 12, 2015

. . . .

Being a Force for Good

I was sitting on television one day doing an interview with the KKK, and I realized in that moment that the energy that I was broadcasting throughout the world was energy that I did not want to be a part of. And so I—literally in the middle of a commercial break—I just thought, "I will never do this again. I will only allow my platform to be used as a force for good."

—*Forbes* 400 Summit on Philanthropy, June 26, 2012

OPRAH'S ACHIEVEMENTS

∙∙

Overcoming Adversity

Some days the awareness of the sanctity and sacredness of life brings me to my knees with gratitude. I'm still trying to wrap my head around the idea that the little girl from Mississippi who grew up holding her nose in an outhouse now flies on her own plane—my own plane!—to Africa to help girls who grew up like her.

—*What I Know For Sure*, p. 160

∙∙

Focusing on Improvement

I don't care about being bigger, because I'm already bigger than I ever expected to be. My constant focus is on being better. Should I be doing multimedia video production? Or seminars on the Internet? How can I do what I'm already doing in a more forceful way?

—*Fortune*, April 1, 2002

• •

Phil Donahue

If there never had been a Phil [Donahue], there never would have been a me. I can talk about things now that I never could have talked about before he came on the air. There's room for both of us.

—New York Times, February 1, 1988

• •

Don't Overreach

I stay in my lane; I know what my lane is.

—interview at Stanford Graduate School of Business,
April 16, 2014

• •

Proceeding with Purpose

When the universe compels me toward the best path to take, it never leaves me with "Maybe," "Should I?" or even "Perhaps." I always know for sure when it's telling me to proceed—because everything inside me rises up to reverberate "Yes!"

—What I Know For Sure, p. 176

....

Journalistic Integrity

But I don't do an interview if someone tells me I can't ask a certain question. My policy is, I can ask any question, you can tell me you won't answer it, but you have to tell me that on camera.

—*The Hollywood Reporter*, December 19, 2012

....

Setting Boundaries after Success

When you're the most successful person in your family, in your neighborhood and in your town, everybody thinks you're the First National Bank and you have to figure out for yourself where those boundaries are.

—*The Hollywood Reporter*, December 11, 2013

....

Controlling Your Brand

In a 1986 interview, Oprah commented that the show did not define her. Over the course of the next 15 years, however, Oprah and her business became inextricably tied:

If I lost control of the business I'd lose myself—or at least the ability to be myself. Owning myself is a way to be myself.

—*Fortune*, April 1, 2002

••

Proving Yourself

I'd just like to be in the space where I really feel like I have nothing to prove.

—*The Hollywood Reporter*, December 11, 2013

••

Empathy

I can relate to pain because I realize all pain is the same. I can relate to being abandoned, I can relate to having people not care about you, I can relate to all of that. All of that helped me be who I am.

—interview with Facebook COO Sheryl Sandberg,
October 2, 2011

••

Relatability

The secret of [*The Oprah Winfrey Show*] for 25 years is that people could see themselves in me. All over the world, they could see themselves in me.

—interview at Stanford Graduate School of Business,
April 16, 2014

•••

Authenticity

My whole career has been based on being truthful in the moment. And if I have to pretend to be interested in something that I'm not interested in, it doesn't work.

—*The Hollywood Reporter*, November 25, 2007

•••

Creating a Phenomenon

I know what it's like to be part of a phenomenon. You can't create a phenomenon. You can't make it. You can't make it happen no matter how many publicity shots you do or how many times you try to get yourself in the press—you cannot create a phenomenon. The people do. It's the people's resonance and response to what it is you're putting out that creates the phenomenon.

—*Oprah Builds a Network*, July 15, 2012

. . . .

Feeling Successful

It's very difficult for me to give myself that credit. It's very difficult for me to even see myself as successful because I still see myself as in the process of becoming successful. To me, "successful" is getting to the point where you are absolutely comfortable with yourself. And it does not matter how many things you have acquired.

—Academy of Achievement, February 21, 1991

. . . .

Money Management

I've been very poor in my life, and so the idea of having money and not being responsible and knowing how much money you have and keeping control of it, is not something that I personally can accept.

—Academy of Achievement, February 21, 1991

. . . .

Being Engaged

The real reward comes when you have true engagement in what it is that you choose to give.

—*Forbes* 400 Summit on Philanthropy, June 26, 2012

A Larger Calling

I always recognized that the life for me and the calling for me was something beyond the expectation that people had in rural Mississippi. So I certainly didn't know that it had a name, or that that name would be talk shows or that [I'd] be in television. I had no idea of that. But I knew that there was something bigger calling me.

—interview with Facebook COO Sheryl Sandberg,
October 2, 2011

Striving for Excellence

Always do the right thing—always. . . . Be excellent. Let excellence be your brand.

—Spelman College Commencement, May 20, 2012

••

Respecting Your Audience

Every day that I stood here [on this stage], I knew that this was exactly where I was supposed to be. And there was many a day . . . like so many of you, I came to work bone tired. . . . But I showed up, because I knew that you were waiting. You were waiting for whatever we had to offer. And that is why I never missed a day, in 25 years, because you were here.

—*The Oprah Winfrey Show*, May 25, 2011

••

Ratings

I don't do anything *just* for ratings, but as I've said, we're in the television business. If you all are not watching this, if this does not attract your attention, then that means we have not succeeded in doing what we're supposed to do as a business. So am I looking for people I am interested in and also that I believe the public is interested in, our viewers? Of course. And does that equal ratings? I hope so.

—*Oprah Builds a Network*, July 15, 2012

· ·

Being Your Own Competition

The reason we were number one for all those years is because we worked harder than everybody else, and we were our number one competition. In the earlier years, every time somebody else would start a show, I would go, "Oh, Geraldo Rivera has a show, oh, Ricki Lake has a show, what are we gonna do?" And I soon learned that I was, and we were, our greatest competition.

—interview with Facebook COO Sheryl Sandberg,
October 2, 2011

· ·

Being Grateful

Opportunities, relationships, even money flowed my way when I learned to be grateful no matter what happened in my life.

—*O, The Oprah Magazine*, November 2000

· ·

Working with the Best

I also believe in excellence—the people I have are excellent.

—*60 Minutes*, December 14, 1986

. . . .

Being Fair

When I first started being a "businesswoman," I worried about, "How do you do this?" And I realized that you do this the same way as you do anything else. You be fair. You try to be honest with other people, and be fair.

—*Academy of Achievement*, February 21, 1991

. . . .

Connecting With Each Other

No doubt, we're all more digitally and fiber-optically linked than ever before, but we're apparently losing our real connections. . . . Listen. Pay attention. . . . Make the connection.

—*O, The Oprah Magazine*, December 2004

. . . .

The Message Is the Key

Ultimately, you have to make money because you are a business. I let other people worry about that. I worry about the message. I am always, always, always about holding true to the vision and the message, and when you are true to that, then people respond.

—*New York Times*, November 25, 2012

· ·

Being a Businesswoman

I didn't have a lot of mentors, you know? I happened into being a businesswoman. It has never been a goal of mine, and I wouldn't necessarily even say it's a strength of mine. . . . I have to really work at it. I have to work at disciplining myself. The business of the business tires me out.

—*The Hollywood Reporter*, November 25, 2007

· ·

The Journey Is the Goal

I think part of the reason I am as successful as I have been is because the success wasn't the goal—the process was. I wanted to do good work. I wanted to do well in my life.

—*60 Minutes*, December 14, 1986

• •

Building to Success

I don't know if anybody really skyrockets to success. I think that success is a process. And I believe that my first Easter speech, at Kosciusko Baptist Church, at the age of three and a half, was the beginning. And that every other speech, every other book I read, every other time I spoke in public, was a building block. So that by the time I first sat down to audition in front of a television camera, and somebody said, "Read this," what allowed me to read it so comfortably and be so at ease with myself at that time, was the fact that I had been doing it a while. If I'd never read a book, or never spoken in public before, I would have been traumatized by it.

—Academy of Achievement, February 21, 1991

• •

Taking a Breath

When I'm mired in confusion about what the next step should be, when I'm asked to do something for which I feel little enthusiasm, that's my sign to just stop—to get still until my instincts give me the go-ahead.

—O, The Oprah Magazine, June 2003

Beating Deadlines

I learned the meaning of excellence in the third grade because I turned in my book report early to my teacher, Mrs. Driver, and she was so impressed with it she told all the other students. They hated me every day afterwards, but it worked wonders with the rest of the teachers.

—*The Hollywood Reporter*, November 25, 2007

It Takes Time

On developing content for OWN:

We're building out one show at a time, 'til we get to 600 and then we'll get to 700 and eventually, 8,000.

—interview with Facebook COO Sheryl Sandberg, October 2, 2011

Limitations

On my own I will just create, and if it works, it works, and if it doesn't, I'll create something else. I don't have any limitations on what I think I could do or be.

—*Forbes*, October 1995

• •

Impact of Oprah's Book Club

One of the most rewarding experiences for me
for the show is opening that world [of reading] to
people. I can't even imagine being 40 years old and
never having read a book, but there were people
who hadn't.

—interview with Barbara Walters, December 9, 2010

• •

Finding Your Place

*Oprah was removed as the co-anchor of the eve-
ning news at Baltimore's WJZ after less than a year
on the job. As she was still under contract, the station moved her around, finally trying her as the co-
host of the talk show* People Are Talking.

It was that failure that led to the talk show. Because
they had no place else to put me, they put me on
a talk show one morning. And I'm telling you, the
hour I interviewed—my very first interview was
the Carvel Ice Cream Man and Benny from "All
My Children"—I'll never forget it. I came off the air
thinking, "This is what I should have been doing,"
because it was like breathing to me. Like breathing. You just talk. "Be yourself" is really what I had
learned to do.

—Academy of Achievement, February 21, 1991

Success Is Not the Goal

What I know for sure is that if you want to have success, you can't make success your goal.

—*O, The Oprah Magazine*, September 2001

Paying Attention

One of my gifts that I've had since I was a little girl, growing up in Mississippi, being raised on a tiny, little acre farm with my grandmother, is that I knew how to pay attention. I was a great observer of life.

—interview at Stanford University, April 20, 2015

Being Original

There won't be a "next Oprah" . . . just like there won't be another Barbara Walters, Aretha Franklin or Whitney Houston. People who make their mark in the way that they made it, that's it.

—*The Hollywood Reporter*, December 11, 2013

••

Knowing Your Business

One of the other big lessons that I've learned, particularly in business, is that you have a responsibility to yourself to learn as much about your business as you can.

—Academy of Achievement, February 21, 1991

••

Being Oprah

I believe in service, I believe in helping people, I want people to feel fulfilled and empowered in their life, but still some days I think, "It's just cool to be me."

—interview with Michelle Obama, June 14, 2016

MILESTONES

1954

Orpah Gail Winfrey (the Biblical "Orpah" was mispronounced as "Oprah" and the name stuck) is born in Kosciusko, Mississippi to Vernita Lee and Vernon Winfrey. She remains in Mississippi with her maternal grandmother for the next six years of her life.

1960

Oprah joins her mother in Milwaukee, Wisconsin. Over the next several years she is sexually abused by members of her family as well as a family friend.

1968

Vernita sends Oprah to Nashville, Tennessee, to live with her father. She gives birth prematurely to a baby boy, who dies shortly afterward.

1971

Oprah lands her first broadcast job at WVOL radio station in Nashville.

1973

Oprah becomes the first female television anchor at WLAC-TV in Nashville.

1976

Oprah moves to Baltimore to co-anchor the six o'clock news for WJZ-TV. She does not get along with her more-established co-anchor and lasts less than a year before she is unceremoniously removed. The station tries her out in different positions and eventually makes her the co-host of the talk show *People Are Talking*.

1984

Oprah makes her Chicago debut as the host of WLS-TV's *AM Chicago*.

1985

Steven Spielberg's *The Color Purple* is released to widespread acclaim. Oprah is nominated for an Academy Award for Best Supporting Actress for her role as Sofia.

AM Chicago is renamed *The Oprah Winfrey Show*.

1986

Oprah forms Harpo, her production company.

The Oprah Winfrey Show goes national.

1987

Oprah wins her first Daytime Emmy Award for Outstanding Talk Show Host; she will go on to be nominated for a further 21 Daytime Emmys, winning 13 as of this book's publication.

1988

Oprah takes full ownership of *The Oprah Winfrey Show*, becoming the first woman in history to own her own talk show.

1991

Oprah testifies in front of the United States Senate Judiciary Committee in support of a national database of convicted child abusers. President Clinton will sign "Oprah's Bill" into law two years later, establishing the database.

Oprah wins Entertainer of the Year at the NAACP Image Awards.

1992

Oprah becomes engaged to Stedman Graham; the couple remains together but they are, as of this book's publication, unwed.

1993

Oprah's prime-time sit-down with Michael Jackson becomes the most-watched interview ever, with over 90 million viewers. The interview is nominated for a Primetime Emmy for Outstanding Informational Special.

1995

Oprah supplants Bill Cosby as the only black American on *Forbes'* 400 wealthiest people list with an estimated net worth of $340 million.

Oprah is awarded a Peabody Personal Award for her on- and off-air accomplishments.

1996

Oprah's Book Club is launched. Selection by the book club becomes a sure indicator of commercial success.

The first episode to feature "Oprah's Favorite Things" airs. The annual show, in which Oprah gives the audience a curated selection of her favorite products for the year, is usually the most-watched show of the season. Items featured on the show routinely receive a large sales boost afterward.

1997

Oprah forms the Angel Network, which supports charitable organizations and provides grants to nonprofits around the world.

1998

Oprah returns to the screen in an adaptation of Toni Morrison's *Beloved*.

Oprah receives the Lifetime Achievement Award from the Academy of Television Arts and Sciences (the Emmy Awards).

2000

O, The Oprah Magazine launches and becomes the most successful magazine start-up.

The NAACP awards Oprah the Spingarn Medal for outstanding achievement by an African American.

2002

Oprah is the inaugural recipient of the Bob Hope Humanitarian Award from the Academy of Television Arts and Sciences for her contributions to television and radio.

2003

Oprah becomes the first female African American billionaire listed in *Forbes'* annual ranking.

2004

Oprah travels to South Africa to film *Oprah's Christmas Kindness*, a show that brings awareness to children affected by poverty and AIDs. Viewers donate over $7 million to the Angel Network in response. Oprah stays with former South African president Nelson Mandela, where she forms the idea to create a school in South Africa for girls.

2005

Forbes names Oprah the world's most powerful celebrity. She will again be #1 in 2007, 2008, 2010, and 2013.

The NAACP Image Awards inducts her into its Hall of Fame.

2006

Oprah launches a new radio station, Oprah Radio, in partnership with XM Satellite Radio. Her contract is worth a reported $55 million for three years.

2007

The Oprah Winfrey Leadership Academy for Girls opens in South Africa. Controversy erupts when several students accuse a dorm matron of physical and sexual abuse. Oprah initiates an independent investigation and flies to South Africa to speak to the students and their parents directly. The dorm matron is eventually acquitted, but Oprah maintains that she believes the girls. Her swift and decisive handling of the incident wins praise by local papers and experts dealing in sexual abuse.

Oprah endorses Barack Obama in the 2008 Democratic presidential primary, marking her first official political endorsement.

2008

Together with Discovery Communications, Oprah creates OWN: The Oprah Winfrey Network. The initial launch date is 2009, but is pushed back to 2011.

In her role as chairwoman of Harpo, *The Hollywood Reporter* names her the most powerful woman in entertainment.

2009

Oprah announces that the 25th season of *The Oprah Winfrey Show* (airing 2010-2011) will be its last.

2010

Oprah is honored by the Kennedy Center for contributions to media.

2011

OWN launches in January. An estimated 505,000 viewers tune in during its first week.

Oprah receives the Jean Hersholt Humanitarian Award from the Academy of Motion Pictures.

OWN CEO Christina Norman is replaced by Discovery executive Peter Ligouri in May after the network fails to gain new viewership.

The last episode of *The Oprah Winfrey Show* airs on May 25th. The episode is watched by an estimated 16.4 million viewers.

Oprah takes over as CEO and chief creative officer of OWN in July.

2012

OWN lays off 20% of its workforce and undergoes further restructuring.

Tyler Perry enters into a partnership with OWN, creating two scripted shows for the network. Perry's original shows become OWN's most consistently watched.

2013

OWN reports that it is profitable for the first time since the channel launched.

Oprah returns to the big screen with a role in *Lee Daniels' The Butler*. She is nominated for several awards, including an NAACP Image Award, BAFTA Award, and SAG award.

Oprah is awarded the Presidential Medal of Freedom.

2014

Forbes ranks Oprah the 14th most powerful woman in the world.

Oprah appears in Ava DuVernay's *Selma*. In her role as an executive producer, she is nominated for an Academy Award for Best Picture, among other awards.

2015

OWN reports four years of positive viewership growth. Perry's shows for OWN routinely draw several million viewers.

Oprah buys a 10% ownership stake in Weight Watchers that includes a seat on its board; its stock price soars in the immediate aftermath.

Oprah announces that her long-awaited memoir, *The Life You Want*, will be published in 2017.

2016

CNN Money reports a surprise $11 million quarterly loss for Weight Watchers, raising questions about the power of Oprah's influence.

Oprah returns to scripted television with OWN's drama *Greenleaf*.

Oprah endorses Hillary Clinton for President.

The Harpo Studios complex in Chicago is demolished, closing that chapter in Oprah's life.

CITATIONS

INTRODUCTION

Oprah Winfrey, interview with Mike Wallace, *60 Minutes*, CBS, December 14, 1986.

PREPARATION

Your Resume Is Your Story

Oprah Winfrey, commencement address at Harvard University, Cambridge, MA, May 30, 2013, https://www.youtube.com/watch?v=GMWFieBGR7c

Luck

Oprah's Master Class. Episode no. 7, first broadcast March 27, 2011 by OWN. Directed by Joe Berlinger.

Don't Waste Time

Oprah Winfrey, "Here We Go!" *O, The Oprah Magazine*, August 2015.

Finding Your Life's Work

Oprah Winfrey, "What I Know for Sure," *O, The Oprah Magazine*, September 2001.

Paying Your Dues

Oprah Builds a Network. Episode no. 1, first broadcast July 8, 2012 by OWN. Directed by Erica Forstadt, written by Jessica Jardine.

Being Present

J.J. McCorvey, "The Key To Oprah Winfrey's Success: Radical Focus." *Fast Company*, October 12, 2015, http://www.fastcompany.com/3051589/secrets-of-the -most-productive-people/the-key-to-oprah-winfreys -success-radical-focus

Being Yourself

Academy of Achievement, "Oprah Winfrey Interview," February 21, 1991, http://www.achievement.org /autodoc/page/winoint-4

Empowering People Face-to-Face

Oprah Builds a Network. Episode no. 1, first broadcast July 8, 2012 by OWN. Directed by Erica Forstadt, written by Jessica Jardine.

Legacy

Oprah Winfrey, interview with Sheryl Sandberg, "The Oprah Facebook Interview," Facebook, Menlo Park, CA, October 2, 2011, http://www.oprah.com/own /The-Oprah-Facebook-Interview.

Running Your Own Race

Oprah's Master Class. Episode no. 7, first broadcast March 27, 2011 by OWN. Directed by Joe Berlinger.

Staying True To Yourself

THR Staff, "The Resurgence of Oprah Winfrey," *The Hollywood Reporter*, December 11, 2013, http://www .hollywoodreporter.com/gallery/resurgence-oprah -winfrey-664696/1-oprah-winfrey.

Expectations

Academy of Achievement, "Oprah Winfrey Interview," February 21, 1991, http://www.achievement.org /autodoc/page/winoint-3.

Success Flows from Service

Oprah Winfrey, "What I Know for Sure," *O, The Oprah Magazine*, September 2001.

Clarity of Purpose

Oprah Winfrey, commencement address at Harvard University, Cambridge, MA, May 30, 2013, https://www.youtube.com/watch?v=GMWFieBGR7c.

Choosing Positive People

Oprah Winfrey, commencement address at Spelman College, Atlanta, GA, May 20, 2012, https://www.youtube.com/watch?v=Bpx8uNzRdew.

Learning from Your Own Life

Oprah Winfrey, interview at Stanford Graduate School of Business, "Oprah Winfrey on Career, Life, and Leadership." Stanford, CA, April 16, 2014, https://www.youtube.com/watch?v=6DlrqeWrczs.

Your Career Is Not Your Life

Oprah Winfrey, "What I Know for Sure," *O, The Oprah Magazine*, April 2014.

Patience

Stacey Wilson Hunt, "Oprah Winfrey on Launching OWN: Lorne Michaels Told Me I'd Use 'Motherf---er' a Lot," *The Hollywood Reporter*, December 19, 2012, http://www.hollywoodreporter.com/news/oprah -winfrey-lorne-michaels-own-404837.

What Goes Around

Oprah Winfrey, interview at Stanford Graduate School of Business, "Oprah Winfrey on Career, Life, and Leadership." Stanford, CA, April 16, 2014, https://www.youtube.com/watch?v=6DlrqeWrczs.

You Are Your Own Best Thing
Brian Stelter, "Oprah Calls and Reflects on 25 Years," *New York Times*, May 24, 2011, http://mediadecoder.blogs .nytimes.com/2011/05/24/oprah-calls-and-reflects-on -25-years.

Nothing Is Guaranteed
Oprah Winfrey, "What I Know for Sure," *O, The Oprah Magazine*, January 2016.

Choosing Who You Want to Be
Oprah Winfrey, "What I Know for Sure," *O, The Oprah Magazine*, April 2014.

Listening to Yourself
Oprah Winfrey, "What I Know for Sure," *O, The Oprah Magazine*, June 2001.

How to Negotiate
THR Staff, "Oprah Winfrey, Shonda Rhimes and 16 Other Hollywood Leaders on How to Negotiate," *The Hollywood Reporter*, December 10, 2015, http://www .hollywoodreporter.com/news/oprah-winfrey-shonda -rhimes-16-846093.

What Successful People Have in Common
The Oprah Winfrey Show. Season 25, episode no. 70, first broadcast May 25, 2011 by ABC. Directed by Joseph C. Terry.

Knowing What You Don't Want
Oprah Winfrey, interview at Stanford Graduate School of Business, "Oprah Winfrey on Career, Life, and Leadership." Stanford, CA, April 16, 2014, https://www.youtube.com/watch?v=6DlrqeWrczs.

Questioning Yourself

Oprah Winfrey, "Here We Go!" *O, The Oprah Magazine*, April 2014.

Your Past Informs Your Present

Oprah Winfrey, interview with Sheryl Sandberg, "The Oprah Facebook Interview," Facebook, Menlo Park, CA, October 2, 2011, http://www.oprah.com/own /The-Oprah-Facebook-Interview.

RISK-TAKING

Using Your Fear

Oprah Winfrey, interview with Sheryl Sandberg, "The Oprah Facebook Interview," Facebook, Menlo Park, CA, October 2, 2011, http://www.oprah.com/own /The-Oprah-Facebook-Interview.

Owning Your Future

Oprah Winfrey, speech at Stanford University, "Harry's Last Lecture," Stanford, CA, April 20, 2015, https://www.youtube.com/watch?v=GR_7X0exvh8.

Taking Advantage of Change

Oprah Winfrey, "What I Know for Sure," *O, The Oprah Magazine*, September 2014.

Being Flexible

Oprah Winfrey, *What I Know For Sure* (New York: Hearst Communications, 2014) p. 35.

Not Playing It Safe

Oprah Winfrey, *What I Know For Sure* (New York: Hearst Communications, 2014) p. 125.

Doing What Is Necessary

Oprah Builds a Network. Episode no. 1, first broadcast
July 8, 2012 by OWN. Directed by Erica Forstadt,
written by Jessica Jardine.

Recalibrating

Oprah Winfrey, "What I Know for Sure," *O, The Oprah
Magazine*, September 2014.

Speaking Out

Jonathan van Meter, "Oprah! A Major Movie, an Amazing
Makeover," *Vogue*, October 1998, http://www.vogue
.com/869933/from-the-archives-oprah-winfrey-in
-vogue.

You're Not Alone

Makers: Women Who Make America. Episode no. 1, first
broadcast February 26, 2013 by PBS. Directed by Barak
Goodman and written by Barak Goodman and Pamela
Mason Wagner.

No Free Rides

Oprah Builds a Network. Episode no. 2, first broadcast
July 15, 2012 by OWN. Directed by Erica Forstadt,
written by Jessica Jardine.

Setting Trends

Brian Stelter, "Oprah Calls and Reflects on 25 Years," *New
York Times*, May 24, 2011, http://mediadecoder.blogs
.nytimes.com/2011/05/24/oprah-calls-and-reflects-on
-25-years.

Being the Boss

Makers: Women Who Make America. Episode no. 1, first
broadcast February 26, 2013 by PBS. Directed by Barak
Goodman and written by Barak Goodman and Pamela
Mason Wagner.

Enjoying the Journey
Oprah Winfrey, "What I Know for Sure," *O, The Oprah Magazine*, February 2001.

Learning from Challenges
Oprah Winfrey, *What I Know For Sure* (New York: Hearst Communications, 2014) p. 44.

Midlife Crisis
Bob Minzesheimer, "Oprah Brings Tolle's 'Earth' to the Classroom," *USA Today*, March 2, 2008, http://usatoday30.usatoday.com/life/people/2008 -03-02-oprah-tolle_N.htm.

Asking for It
Oprah Winfrey, "Here We Go!" *O, The Oprah Magazine*, July 2014.

Moving On
Oprah Winfrey, *What I Know For Sure* (New York: Hearst Communications, 2014) p. 103.

DECISION-MAKING

Finding Your Purpose
Oprah Winfrey, commencement address at Spelman College, Atlanta, GA, May 20, 2012, https://www .youtube.com/watch?v=Bpx8uNzRdew.

Knowing When to Quit
Lacey Rose, "The Resurgence of Oprah Winfrey," *The Hollywood Reporter*, December 11, 2013, http://www .hollywoodreporter.com/news/oprah-winfrey -forgoing-motherhood-being-664550 .

Honoring Yourself

Oprah Winfrey, "What I Know for Sure," *O, The Oprah Magazine*, June 2001.

Layoffs

Oprah Builds a Network. Episode no. 2, first broadcast July 15, 2012 by OWN. Directed by Erica Forstadt, written by Jessica Jardine.

Listening to Your Instincts

Oprah Winfrey, interview at Stanford Graduate School of Business, "Oprah Winfrey on Career, Life, and Leadership." Stanford, CA, April 16, 2014, https://www.youtube.com/watch?v=6DlrqeWrczs.

Strategic-Planning Meetings

Patricia Sellers, "The Business of Being Oprah," *Fortune*, April 1, 2002, http://archive.fortune.com/magazines /fortune/fortune_archive/2002/04/01/320634/index .htm.

Asking the Right Questions

Oprah Winfrey, "What I Know for Sure," *O, The Oprah Magazine*, April 2014.

Multitasking

J.J. McCorvey, "The Key To Oprah Winfrey's Success: Radical Focus," *Fast Company*, October 12, 2015, http://www.fastcompany.com/3051589/secrets-of-the -most-productive-people/the-key-to-oprah-winfreys -success-radical-focus.

Listening to Your Uncertainty

Oprah Winfrey, *What I Know For Sure* (New York: Hearst Communications, 2014) p. 176.

Waiting for Clarity

Oprah Winfrey, *What I Know For Sure* (New York: Hearst Communications, 2014) p. 215.

Planning Ahead

Oprah Winfrey, "What I Know for Sure," *O, The Oprah Magazine*, April 2015.

Removing Your Fear

Oprah Winfrey, *What I Know For Sure* (New York: Hearst Communications, 2014) p. 39.

Listening to Your Inner Voice

Oprah Winfrey, interview at Stanford Graduate School of Business, "Oprah Winfrey on Career, Life, and Leadership." Stanford, CA, April 16, 2014, https://www.youtube.com/watch?v=6DlrqeWrczs.

CHALLENGES

Rough Patches

Oprah Winfrey, "Here We Go!" *O, The Oprah Magazine*, August 2014.

There's No Such Thing as Failure

Oprah Winfrey, commencement address at Harvard University, Cambridge, MA, May 30, 2013, https://www.youtube.com/watch?v=GMWFieBGR7c.

Learning from Your Critics

Academy of Achievement, "Oprah Winfrey Interview," February 21, 1991, http://www.achievement.org /autodoc/page/winoint-5.

Mistakes Are Teachable Moments

Oprah Winfrey, commencement address at Harvard
University, Cambridge, MA, May 30, 2013,
https://www.youtube.com/watch?v=GMWFieBGR7c.

Disagreements

Oprah Winfrey, interview at Stanford Graduate School
of Business, "Oprah Winfrey on Career, Life, and
Leadership." Stanford, CA, April 16, 2014,
https://www.youtube.com/watch?v=6DlrqeWrczs.

Setting Expectations

Oprah Winfrey, interview with Charlie Rose, Gayle King,
and Norah O'Donnell, *CBS This Morning*, CBS, first
broadcast April 2, 2012, https://www.youtube.com
/watch?v=XUfO3-wQLc8.

Don't Rest on Your Laurels

Stacey Wilson Hunt, "Oprah Winfrey on Launching
OWN: Lorne Michaels Told Me I'd Use 'Motherf---er'
a Lot," *The Hollywood Reporter*, December 19, 2012,
http://www.hollywoodreporter.com/news/oprah
-winfrey-lorne-michaels-own-404837.

Being Lean

Christopher S. Stewart, "Oprah Struggles to Build Her
Network," *Wall Street Journal*, May 6, 2012,
http://www.wsj.com/articles/SB1000142405270230474
6604577382101741961484.

Pleasing Others

Academy of Achievement, "Oprah Winfrey Interview,"
February 21, 1991, http://www.achievement.org
/autodoc/page/winoint-6.

Maintaining Control

Brian Stelter, "Oprah's Network Is Her Highest Hurdle," *New York Times*, December 18, 2010, http://www .nytimes.com/2010/12/19/business/19oprah.html.

Schadenfreude

Oprah Builds a Network. Episode no. 2, first broadcast July 15, 2012 by OWN. Directed by Erica Forstadt, written by Jessica Jardine.

Finding Higher Ground

Oprah Winfrey, *What I Know For Sure* (New York: Hearst Communications, 2014) p. 35.

New Directions

Oprah Winfrey, *What I Know For Sure* (New York: Hearst Communications, 2014) p. 46.

Stepping Out of Your Ego

Oprah Winfrey, *What I Know For Sure* (New York: Hearst Communications, 2014) p. 42.

Listening to Life

Kunbi Tinuoye, "Oprah Winfrey, Still the Real Deal," *Ebony*, September 11, 2014, http://www.ebony.com /entertainment-culture/oprah-winfrey-still-the-real -deal-987.

WORK/LIFE BALANCE

Fun

Oprah Winfrey, "What I Know for Sure," *O, The Oprah Magazine*, February 2015.

Avoiding Negativity

Oprah Winfrey, *What I Know For Sure* (New York: Hearst Communications, 2014) p. 186.

Dysfunction

Oprah Winfrey, interview with Michelle Obama at
United State of Women Summit, "First Lady Michelle
Obama and Oprah Winfrey Hold a Conversation on
the Next Generation of Women," Washington DC,
June 14, 2016.

Learning to Say No

Academy of Achievement, "Oprah Winfrey Interview,"
February 21, 1991, http://www.achievement.org
/autodoc/page/winoint-4.

Time

Oprah Winfrey, *What I Know For Sure* (New York: Hearst
Communications, 2014) p. 178.

Protecting Your Light

Oprah Winfrey, *What I Know For Sure* (New York: Hearst
Communications, 2014) p. 186.

Not Having Children

Oprah Winfrey, interview with Barbara Walters,
Nightline, ABC, first broadcast December 9, 2010.

Taking Breaks

Oprah Winfrey, *What I Know For Sure* (New York: Hearst
Communications, 2014) p. 181.

Work Day

Academy of Achievement, "Oprah Winfrey Interview,"
February 21, 1991, http://www.achievement.org
/autodoc/page/winoint-8.

Silence

Oprah Winfrey, "What I Know for Sure," *O, The Oprah
Magazine*, October 2014.

Turning Down Requests

Oprah Winfrey, speech at Stanford University, "Harry's Last Lecture," Stanford, CA, April 20, 2015, https://www.youtube.com/watch?v=GR_7Xoexvh8.

Leaving Space in Your Calendar

Oprah Winfrey, *What I Know For Sure* (New York: Hearst Communications, 2014) p. 180.

Relaxation

Oprah Winfrey, "Here We Go!" *O, The Oprah Magazine*, July 2015.

Finding Balance

Oprah Winfrey, *What I Know For Sure* (New York: Hearst Communications, 2014) p. 6.

Staying Refreshed

Oprah Winfrey, "Here We Go!" *O, The Oprah Magazine*, September 2014.

Happiness

Patricia Sellers, "The Business of Being Oprah," *Fortune*, April 1, 2002, http://archive.fortune.com/magazines/fortune/fortune_archive/2002/04/01/320634/index.htm.

Time Management

Oprah Winfrey, "What I Know for Sure," *O, The Oprah Magazine*, June 2015.

Fresh Starts

Oprah Winfrey, *What I Know For Sure* (New York: Hearst Communications, 2014) p. 24.

Prioritizing Yourself

Oprah Winfrey, "What I Know for Sure," *O, The Oprah Magazine*, June 2015.

Remembering to Breathe

Oprah Winfrey, *What I Know For Sure* (New York: Hearst
　　Communications, 2014) p. 170.

Focusing on the Present

Oprah Winfrey, *What I Know For Sure* (New York: Hearst
　　Communications, 2014) p. 167.

LEADERSHIP

Owning Your Vision

Stacey Wilson Hunt, "Oprah Winfrey on Launching
　　OWN: Lorne Michaels Told Me I'd Use 'Motherf---er'
　　a Lot," *The Hollywood Reporter*, December 19, 2012,
　　http://www.hollywoodreporter.com/news/oprah
　　-winfrey-lorne-michaels-own-404837.

Pursuing Excellence

Oprah Winfrey, *What I Know For Sure* (New York: Hearst
　　Communications, 2014) p. 126.

Humility

Oprah Winfrey, interview at Stanford Graduate School
　　of Business, "Oprah Winfrey on Career, Life, and
　　Leadership." Stanford, CA, April 16, 2014,
　　https://www.youtube.com/watch?v=6DlrqeWrczs.

Showing Up

Oprah Winfrey, interview with Barbara Walters, *Oprah:
　　The Next Chapter*, ABC, first broadcast December 9,
　　2010.

Creating the Culture

Oprah Winfrey, interview with Sheryl Sandberg, "The
　　Oprah Facebook Interview," Facebook, Menlo Park,
　　CA, October 2, 2011, http://www.oprah.com/own
　　/The-Oprah-Facebook-Interview.

Hiring the Right People

J.J. McCorvey, "The Key To Oprah Winfrey's Success: Radical Focus," *Fast Company*, October 12, 2015, http://www.fastcompany.com/3051589/secrets-of-the-most-productive-people/the-key-to-oprah-winfreys-success-radical-focus.

Envisioning the Future

Oprah Winfrey, "What I Know for Sure," *O, The Oprah Magazine*, May 2015.

Sharing Intentions

Oprah Winfrey, interview with Jeff Weiner, "My Interview with Oprah," LinkedIn.com, October 15, 2015, https://www.linkedin.com/pulse/my-interview-oprah-jeff-weiner

Sending a Message

Makers: Women Who Make America. Episode no. 1, first broadcast February 26, 2013 by PBS. Directed by Barak Goodman and written by Barak Goodman and Pamela Mason Wagner.

Taking Control

Oprah Builds a Network. Episode no. 1, first broadcast July 8, 2012 by OWN. Directed by Erica Forstadt, written by Jessica Jardine.

Holding High Expectations

Christy Crosz and Stephen Galloway, "A Dialogue with Oprah Winfrey," *The Hollywood Reporter*, November 25, 2007, http://www.hollywoodreporter.com/new/dialogue-oprah-winfrey-155660.

Integrity in Action

Oprah Winfrey, interview with Moira Forbes, *Forbes* 400 Summit on Philanthropy, New York, NY, June 26, 2012, https://www.youtube.com/watch?v=ovpgi4Ijquo.

Developing Talent

Oprah Winfrey, interview with Barbara Walters, *Oprah: The Next Chapter*, ABC, first broadcast December 9, 2010.

Creating a Team

Oprah Winfrey, interview with Sheryl Sandberg, "The Oprah Facebook Interview," Facebook, Menlo Park, CA, October 2, 2011, http://www.oprah.com/own /The-Oprah-Facebook-Interview.

Working Together

Oprah Winfrey, interview with Charlie Rose, Gayle King, and Norah O'Donnell, *CBS This Morning*, CBS, first broadcast August 5, 2013, http://www.cbs.com/shows /cbs_this_morning/video/yPjxgHjx7gghbBPJNXojOe8 po7drfkiA/oprah-reflects-own-success-o-magazine -and-more.

Sharing the Load

Oprah Winfrey, interview with Sheryl Sandberg, "The Oprah Facebook Interview," Facebook, Menlo Park, CA, October 2, 2011, http://www.oprah.com/own /The-Oprah-Facebook-Interview.

Courage

Oprah Winfrey, "What I Know for Sure," *O, The Oprah Magazine*, January 2015.

Personal Growth

The Oprah Winfrey Show. Season 25, episode no. 70, first broadcast May 25, 2011 by ABC. Directed by Joseph C. Terry.

Raising Consciousness
Oprah Winfrey, interview at Stanford Graduate School of Business, "Oprah Winfrey on Career, Life, and Leadership." Stanford, CA, April 16, 2014, https://www.youtube.com/watch?v=6DlrqeWrczs.

Honesty under Fire
Oprah Winfrey, press conference regarding alleged abuse at the school, The Oprah Winfrey Leadership Academy for Girls, South Africa, November 5, 2007, http://images.oprah.com/download/pdfs/about /events/about_owla.pdf.

Shared Vision, Shared Passion
Oprah Winfrey, interview with Moira Forbes, *Forbes* 400 Summit on Philanthropy, New York, NY, June 26, 2012, https://www.youtube.com/watch?v=ovpgi4Ijquo.

Figuring Out What Works
Oprah Builds a Network. Episode no. 1, first broadcast July 8, 2012 by OWN. Directed by Erica Forstadt, written by Jessica Jardine.

Meetings
J.J. McCorvey, "The Key To Oprah Winfrey's Success: Radical Focus," *Fast Company*, October 12, 2015, http://www.fastcompany.com/3051589/secrets-of-the -most-productive-people/the-key-to-oprah-winfreys -success-radical-focus.

Thinking Big
Patricia Sellers, "Oprah's Next Act," *Fortune*, September 30, 2010, http://archive.fortune.com/2010/09/29 /news/companies/oprah_most_powerful_full.fortune /index.htm.

Running a Business

Christy Crosz and Stephen Galloway, "A Dialogue with Oprah Winfrey," *The Hollywood Reporter*, November 25, 2007, http://www.hollywoodreporter.com/news /dialogue-oprah-winfrey-155660.

Fostering Hope

Oprah Winfrey, interview at Stanford Graduate School of Business, "Oprah Winfrey on Career, Life, and Leadership." Stanford, CA, April 16, 2014, https://www.youtube.com/watch?v=6DlrqeWrczs.

Putting the Right People in Charge

Stephen Galloway, "Oprah in Her Own Words," *The Hollywood Reporter*, May 26, 2011, http://www .hollywoodreporter.com/news/oprah-her-own -words-191633.

Intention

Oprah Winfrey, interview with Jeff Weiner, "My Interview with Oprah," LinkedIn.com, October 15, 2015, https://www.linkedin.com/pulse/my-interview -oprah-jeff-weiner

Leading by Example

Oprah Winfrey, *What I Know For Sure* (New York: Hearst Communications, 2014) p. 200.

Serving Others

Oprah Winfrey, interview with Jeff Weiner, "My Interview with Oprah," LinkedIn.com, October 15, 2015, https://www.linkedin.com/pulse/my-interview -oprah-jeff-weiner

Taking Responsibility

Oprah Winfrey, press conference regarding alleged abuse at the school, The Oprah Winfrey Leadership Academy for Girls, South Africa, November 5, 2007, http://images.oprah.com/download/pdfs/about/events/about_owla.pdf.

Trusting Your People

Lynette Rice, "Oprah Winfrey on OWN," *Entertainment Weekly*, May 6, 2011, http://www.ew.com/article/2011/05/06/oprah-winfrey-own.

Self Reflection

Oprah Winfrey, interview at Stanford Graduate School of Business, "Oprah Winfrey on Career, Life, and Leadership." Stanford, CA, April 16, 2014, https://www.youtube.com/watch?v=6DlrqeWrczs.

Leading Through Transitions

Oprah Winfrey, "What I Know for Sure," *O, The Oprah Magazine*, May 2015.

Sharing Opportunity

Debra Birnbaum, "Oprah Winfrey on Her Journey from Talk Show Royalty to 'Real Freedom,'" *Variety*, October 6, 2015, http://variety.com/2015/tv/news/oprah-winfrey-own-harpo-1201610642.

Leveraging Your Strengths

The Oprah Winfrey Show. Season 25, episode no. 70, first broadcast May 25, 2011 by ABC. Directed by Joseph C. Terry.

MISSION, VISION, AND PHILANTHROPY

Inspiring Others with Your Mission

Christy Crosz and Stephen Galloway, "A Dialogue with Oprah Winfrey," *The Hollywood Reporter*, November 25, 2007, http://www.hollywoodreporter.com/news /dialogue-oprah-winfrey-155660.

Service to Others

Oprah Winfrey, convocation address Northwestern University Kellogg School of Management, Evanston, IL, June 16, 2001, https://www.kellogg.northwestern. edu/kwo/sumo1/inbrief/grad2001.htm.

Sharing Your Vision

The Oprah Winfrey Show. Season 25, episode no. 70, first broadcast May 25, 2011 by ABC. Directed by Joseph C. Terry.

Finding Your Calling

The Oprah Winfrey Show. Season 25, episode no. 70, first broadcast May 25, 2011 by ABC. Directed by Joseph C. Terry.

Developing a Platform

Oprah Winfrey, interview with Jeff Weiner, "My Interview with Oprah," LinkedIn.com, October 15, 2015, https://www.linkedin.com/pulse/my-interview -oprah-jeff-weiner

Following Your Own Lead

Oprah Winfrey, interview with Sheryl Sandberg, "The Oprah Facebook Interview," Facebook, Menlo Park, CA, October 2, 2011, http://www.oprah.com/own /The-Oprah-Facebook-Interview.

Brand

Oprah Winfrey, interview with Moira Forbes, *Forbes* 400 Summit on Philanthropy, New York, NY, June 26, 2012, https://www.youtube.com/watch?v=ovpgi4Ijquo.

OWN's Philosophy

Oprah Winfrey, interview with Sheryl Sandberg, "The Oprah Facebook Interview," Facebook, Menlo Park, CA, October 2, 2011, http://www.oprah.com/own /The-Oprah-Facebook-Interview.

Education Is Liberation

Academy of Achievement, "Oprah Winfrey Interview," February 21, 1991, http://www.achievement.org /autodoc/page/winoint-7.

Doing Comes from Being

Oprah Winfrey, interview at Stanford Graduate School of Business, "Oprah Winfrey on Career, Life, and Leadership." Stanford, CA, April 16, 2014, https://www.youtube.com/watch?v=6DlrqeWrczs.

Having Vision

Oprah Winfrey, interview with Moira Forbes, *Forbes* 400 Summit on Philanthropy, New York, NY, June 26, 2012, https://www.youtube.com/watch?v=ovpgi4Ijquo.

Changing Lives

Academy of Achievement, "Oprah Winfrey Interview," February 21, 1991, http://www.achievement.org /autodoc/page/winoint-2.

Surrendering to Your Dream

Oprah Winfrey, "What I Know for Sure," *O, The Oprah Magazine*, September 2001.

Living in the Moment

Tom Gliatto, "A Party from the Heart," *People*, May 30, 2005, http://www.people.com/people/archive/article /0,,20147698,00.html.

What Really Matters

The Oprah Winfrey Show. Season 25, episode no. 70, first broadcast May 25, 2011 by ABC. Directed by Joseph C. Terry.

Lightening Up

Oprah Builds a Network. Episode no. 1, first broadcast July 8, 2012 by OWN. Directed by Erica Forstadt, written by Jessica Jardine.

Sharing

Oprah Winfrey, interview with Moira Forbes, *Forbes* 400 Summit on Philanthropy, New York, NY, June 26, 2012, https://www.youtube.com/watch?v=0vpgi4Ijquo.

Being Kind

Oprah Winfrey, commencement address at Harvard University, Cambridge, MA, May 30, 2013, https://www.youtube.com/watch?v=GMWFieBGR7c.

Female Education

Oprah Winfrey, interview with Sheryl Sandberg, "The Oprah Facebook Interview," Facebook, Menlo Park, CA, October 2, 2011, http://www.oprah.com/own /The-Oprah-Facebook-Interview.

Feminism

Makers: Women Who Make America. Episode no. 1, first broadcast February 26, 2013 by PBS. Directed by Barak Goodman and written by Barak Goodman and Pamela Mason Wagner.

Civil Rights Movement

Oprah Winfrey, interview by Kelly Ripa and Michael Strahan, *Live with Kelly and Michael*, ABC, December 19, 2014, https://www.youtube.com /watch?v=kGeQB4aEl80.

Gratitude

Oprah Winfrey, "What I Know for Sure," *O, The Oprah Magazine*, December 2013.

Finding Your Passion

Oprah Winfrey, "What I Know for Sure," *O, The Oprah Magazine*, September 2001.

Philanthropy

Debra Birnbaum, "Oprah Winfrey Works to Break the Poverty Cycle Through Education," *Variety*, October 6, 2015, http://variety.com/2015/tv/news/oprah-winfrey -leadership-academy-poverty-1201610760/.

Material Success

Academy of Achievement, "Oprah Winfrey Interview," February 21, 1991, http://www.achievement.org /autodoc/page/winoint-7.

Education Opens Doors

Debra Birnbaum, "Oprah Winfrey Works to Break the Poverty Cycle Through Education," *Variety*, October 6, 2015, http://variety.com/2015/tv/news/oprah-winfrey -leadership-academy-poverty-1201610760/.

Recognizing When You've Made It

Oprah Winfrey, "What I Know for Sure," *O, The Oprah Magazine*, September 2001.

Books

Patricia Sellers, "The Business of Being Oprah," *Fortune*, April 1, 2002, http://archive.fortune.com/magazines /fortune/fortune_archive/2002/04/01/320634/index .htm.

Inspiration

Oprah Winfrey, interview at Stanford Graduate School of Business, "Oprah Winfrey on Career, Life, and Leadership." Stanford, CA, April 16, 2014, https://www.youtube.com/watch?v=6DlrqeWrczs.

We Are All Alike

Jonathan van Meter, "Oprah! A Major Movie, an Amazing Makeover," *Vogue*, October 1998, http://www.vogue. com/869933/from-the-archives-oprah-winfrey-in -vogue.

OWN's Mission

Oprah Winfrey, interview with Charlie Rose, Gayle King, and Norah O'Donnell, *CBS This Morning*, CBS, first broadcast April 2, 2012, https://www.youtube.com /watch?v=XUfO3-wQLc8.

Giving Your Truth

Oprah Winfrey, interview with Moira Forbes, *Forbes* 400 Summit on Philanthropy, New York, NY, June 26, 2012, https://www.youtube.com/watch?v=ovpgi4Ijquo.

Empowering Others

Oprah Winfrey, interview with Jeff Weiner, "My Interview with Oprah," LinkedIn.com, October 15, 2015, https://www.linkedin.com/pulse/my-interview -oprah-jeff-weiner

Changing Perspectives

Oprah Winfrey, interview with Moira Forbes, *Forbes* 400 Summit on Philanthropy, New York, NY, June 26, 2012, https://www.youtube.com/watch?v=ovpgi4Ijquo.

Providing Inspiration

J.J. McCorvey, "The Key To Oprah Winfrey's Success: Radical Focus." *Fast Company*, October 12, 2015, http://www.fastcompany.com/3051589/secrets-of-the-most-productive-people/the-key-to-oprah-winfreys-success-radical-focus.

Being a Force for Good

Oprah Winfrey, interview with Moira Forbes, *Forbes* 400 Summit on Philanthropy, New York, NY, June 26, 2012, https://www.youtube.com/watch?v=ovpgi4Ijquo.

OPRAH'S ACHIEVEMENTS

Overcoming Adversity

Oprah Winfrey, *What I Know For Sure* (New York: Hearst Communications, 2014) p. 160.

Focusing on Improvement

Patricia Sellers, "The Business of Being Oprah," *Fortune*, April 1, 2002, http://archive.fortune.com/magazines/fortune/fortune_archive/2002/04/01/320634/index.htm.

Phil Donahue

Nan Robertson, "Donahue vs. Winfrey: A Class of Talk Titans," *New York Times*, February 1, 1988, http://www.nytimes.com/1988/02/01/arts/donahue-vs-winfrey-a-clash-of-talk-titans.html.

Don't Overreach

Oprah Winfrey, interview at Stanford Graduate School of Business, "Oprah Winfrey on Career, Life, and Leadership." Stanford, CA, April 16, 2014, https://www.youtube.com/watch?v=6DlrqeWrczs.

Proceeding with Purpose

Oprah Winfrey, *What I Know For Sure* (New York: Hearst Communications, 2014) p. 176.

Journalistic Integrity

Stacey Wilson Hunt, "Oprah Winfrey on Launching OWN: Lorne Michaels Told Me I'd Use 'Motherf---er' a Lot," *The Hollywood Reporter*, December 19, 2012, http://www.hollywoodreporter.com/news/oprah-winfrey-lorne-michaels-own-404837.

Setting Boundaries after Success

THR Staff, "The Resurgence of Oprah Winfrey," *The Hollywood Reporter*, December 11, 2013, http://www.hollywoodreporter.com/gallery/resurgence-oprah-winfrey-664696/1-oprah-winfrey.

Controlling Your Brand

Patricia Sellers, "The Business of Being Oprah," *Fortune*, April 1, 2002, http://archive.fortune.com/magazines/fortune/fortune_archive/2002/04/01/320634/index.htm.

Proving Yourself

THR Staff, "The Resurgence of Oprah Winfrey," *The Hollywood Reporter*, December 11, 2013, http://www.hollywoodreporter.com/gallery/resurgence-oprah-winfrey-664696/1-oprah-winfrey.

Empathy

Oprah Winfrey, interview with Sheryl Sandberg, "The Oprah Facebook Interview," Facebook, Menlo Park, CA, October 2, 2011, http://www.oprah.com/own /The-Oprah-Facebook-Interview.

Relatability

Oprah Winfrey, interview at Stanford Graduate School of Business, "Oprah Winfrey on Career, Life, and Leadership." Stanford, CA, April 16, 2014, https://www.youtube.com/watch?v=6DlrqeWrczs.

Authenticity

Christy Crosz and Stephen Galloway, "A Dialogue with Oprah Winfrey," *The Hollywood Reporter*, November 25, 2007, http://www.hollywoodreporter.com/news /dialogue-oprah-winfrey-155660.

Creating a Phenomenon

Oprah Builds a Network. Episode no. 2, first broadcast July 15, 2012 by OWN. Directed by Erica Forstadt, written by Jessica Jardine.

Feeling Successful

Academy of Achievement, "Oprah Winfrey Interview," February 21, 1991, http://www.achievement.org /autodoc/page/winoint-4.

Money Management

Academy of Achievement, "Oprah Winfrey Interview." February 21, 1991, http://www.achievement.org /autodoc/page/winoint-8.

Being Engaged

Oprah Winfrey, interview with Moira Forbes, *Forbes* 400 Summit on Philanthropy, New York, NY, June 26, 2012, https://www.youtube.com/watch?v=0vpgi4Ijqu0.

A Larger Calling

Oprah Winfrey, interview with Sheryl Sandberg, "The Oprah Facebook Interview," Facebook, Menlo Park, CA, October 2, 2011, http://www.oprah.com/own /The-Oprah-Facebook-Interview.

Striving for Excellence

Oprah Winfrey, commencement address at Spelman College, Atlanta, GA, May 20, 2012, https://www .youtube.com/watch?v=Bpx8uNzRdew.

Respecting Your Audience

The Oprah Winfrey Show. Season 25, episode no. 70, first broadcast May 25, 2011 by ABC. Directed by Joseph C. Terry.

Ratings

Oprah Builds a Network. Episode no. 2, first broadcast July 15, 2012 by OWN. Directed by Erica Forstadt, written by Jessica Jardine.

Being Your Own Competition

Oprah Winfrey, interview with Sheryl Sandberg, "The Oprah Facebook Interview," Facebook, Menlo Park, CA, October 2, 2011, http://www.oprah.com/own /The-Oprah-Facebook-Interview.

Being Grateful

Oprah Winfrey, "What I Know for Sure," *O, The Oprah Magazine*, November 2000.

Working with the Best

Oprah Winfrey, interview with Mike Wallace, *60 Minutes*, CBS, December 14, 1986.

Being Fair

Academy of Achievement, "Oprah Winfrey Interview,"
February 21, 1991, http://www.achievement.org
/autodoc/page/winoint-8.

Connecting With Each Other

Oprah Winfrey, "What I Know for Sure," *O, The Oprah
Magazine*, December 2004.

The Message Is the Key

Christine Haughney, "Oprah at a Crossroads," *New York
Times*, November 25, 2012, http://www.nytimes.
com/2012/11/26/business/media/oprah-winfrey-seeks
-to-bolster-a-flagging-empire.html.

Being a Businesswoman

Christy Crosz and Stephen Galloway, "A Dialogue with
Oprah Winfrey," *The Hollywood Reporter*, November
25, 2007, http://www.hollywoodreporter.com/news
/dialogue-oprah-winfrey-155660.

The Journey Is the Goal

Oprah Winfrey, interview with Mike Wallace, *60
Minutes*, CBS, December 14, 1986.

Building to Success

Academy of Achievement, "Oprah Winfrey Interview,"
February 21, 1991, http://www.achievement.org
/autodoc/page/winoint-4.

Taking a Breath

Oprah Winfrey, "What I Know for Sure," *O, The Oprah
Magazine*, June 2003.

Beating Deadlines

Christy Crosz and Stephen Galloway, "A Dialogue with Oprah Winfrey," *Hollywood Reporter*, November 25, 2007, http://www.hollywoodreporter.com/news /dialogue-oprah-winfrey-155660.

It Takes Time

Oprah Winfrey, interview with Sheryl Sandberg, "The Oprah Facebook Interview," Facebook, Menlo Park, CA, October 2, 2011, http://www.oprah.com/own /The-Oprah-Facebook-Interview.

Limitations

Robert La Franco with Josh McHugh, "How Oprah Went From Talk Show Host to First African-American Woman Billionaire," *Forbes*, October 1995, http://www .forbes.com/sites/jennifereum/2014/09/29/how-oprah -went-from-talk-show-host-to-first-african-american -woman-billionaire/#3427957db650.

Impact of Oprah's Book Club

Oprah Winfrey, interview with Barbara Walters, *Oprah: The Next Chapter*, ABC, first broadcast December 9, 2010.

Finding Your Place

Academy of Achievement, "Oprah Winfrey Interview," February 21, 1991, http://www.achievement.org /autodoc/page/winoint-5.

Success Is Not the Goal

Oprah Winfrey, "What I Know for Sure," *O, The Oprah Magazine*, September 2001.

Paying Attention

Oprah Winfrey, speech at Stanford University, "Harry's Last Lecture," Stanford, CA, April 20, 2015, https://www.youtube.com/watch?v=GR_7X0exvh8.

Being Original

THR Staff, "The Resurgence of Oprah Winfrey," *The Hollywood Reporter*, December 11, 2013, http://www.hollywoodreporter.com/gallery/resurgence-oprah-winfrey-664696/1-oprah-winfrey.

Knowing Your Business

Academy of Achievement, "Oprah Winfrey Interview," February 21, 1991, http://www.achievement.org/autodoc/page/winoint-8.

Being Oprah

Oprah Winfrey, interview with Michelle Obama at United State of Women Summit, "First Lady Michelle Obama and Oprah Winfrey Hold a Conversation on the Next Generation of Women," Washington DC, June 14, 2016.

ABOUT THE EDITORS

Anjali Becker is a writer and editor living in Kuala Lumpur, Malaysia. She previously worked as the publicity coordinator for a publisher in Illinois.

Jeanne Engelmann is a writer and editor living in St. Paul, Minnesota. She previously worked as a senior copywriter and art director for a publishing company. She is also the author of several books, curricula, and other educational materials.